Going for

Books to change your life and work.
Accessible, easy to read and easy to act on –
other titles in the **How To** series include

Asserting Your Self
How to feel confident about getting more from life

Self-Counselling
How to develop the skills to positively manage your own life

Discovering Meditation
How to practise meditation techniques to find inner calm and resolution

Using Relaxation for Health and Success
Stress reducing techniques for confidence and positive health

Building Self-Esteem
How to replace self-doubt with confidence and well-being

Learning to Counsel
How to develop the skills to work effectively with others

The *How To Series* now contains
around 200 titles in the following categories:

Business & Management
Computer Basics
General Reference
Jobs & Careers
Living & Working Abroad
Personal Finance
Self-Development
Small Business
Student Handbooks
Successful Writing

For full details, please send for a free copy
of the latest catalogue to:

How To Books
Customers Services Dept.
Plymbridge Distributors Ltd, Estover Road
Plymouth PL6 7PZ, United Kingdom
Tel: 01752 202301   Fax: 01752 202331
http://www.howtobooks.co.uk

Going for
Counselling

*Working with a counsellor to
develop essential life skills*

**WILLIAM STEWART
AND ANGELA MARTIN**

How To Books

Published in 1999 by
How To Books Ltd, 3 Newtec Place,
Magdalen Road, Oxford OX4 1RE, United Kingdom.
Tel: (01865) 793806. Fax: (01865) 248780.
email: info@howtobooks.co.uk
http://www.howtobooks.co.uk

British Library Cataloguing in Publication Data.
A catalogue record for this book is available from
the British Library.

Edited by Diana Brueton
Cover design by Shireen Nathoo
Cover image by PhtoDisc

Produced for How To Books by Deer Park Productions
Typeset by Kestrel Data, Exeter
Printed and bound by Cromwell Press Ltd, Trowbridge, Wiltshire

NOTE: The material contained in this book is set out in good
faith for general guidance and no liability can be accepted
for loss or expense incurred as a result of relying in particular
circumstances on statements made in the book. Laws and
regulations are complex and liable to change, and readers should
check the current position with the relevant authorities before
making personal arrangements.

Contents

Preface

This book is written with the fundamental belief that the more you know about counselling before you start, the more you will gain from it. When you are in counselling, the greater the understanding you have of the process, the more you will get out of it.

However, you may be wary of counselling. We often fear what we do not know, or have no experience of. If you have a problem with your car, you visit a mechanic; a problem with your waste disposal, you call in a plumber. If you are experiencing emotional difficulties, why not go for counselling?

This book aims to demystify counselling; to demonstrate what could take place within the privacy of the counselling room. The principal theme is that you, the client, have a crucial part to play in what happens. Indeed everything hinges on the interaction between you and your counsellor, for without you there would be no counselling. Thus one theme that runs all the way through the book is that of partnership, and that means you and your counsellor working closely together.

Counsellors specialise in working with people who are experiencing emotional difficulties. Going for counselling does not mean that you are weak-willed. Neither does it mean that you are mentally ill. What it does mean is that you have hit a patch in your life where your normal coping skills do not seem strong enough to see you through. Counsellors often need counselling too.

Stress, bereavement, relationship difficulties and depression are some of the common problems for which an increasing number of people seek counselling. Others may not have any specific problem or difficulty, and choose counselling as one way of getting to know themselves. Over the years we have become used to such terms as self-awareness, self-actualisation and personal growth. What all of these, and the many techniques connected with them, have in common, is more understanding of what makes us tick.

Not all counselling is problem-centred. Getting to know yourself – gaining insight – is an essential part of any counselling, though this does not mean that at the end of counselling you will know yourself thoroughly. Becoming more self-aware is a lifetime process. Counselling can help you know more about your personality, the way you relate to people, your strengths and weaknesses, the way you think, feel and behave, and introduce you to ways in which you can develop strategies to manage your life more effectively.

Counselling can bring rewards in many areas of life. Personal and work relationships can take on new meaning. It can help you to become more understanding of yourself and other people. You may find or develop strengths that have lain dormant. You may find you have a greater ability to solve problems and deal with stress more effectively. Many people who have engaged in counselling speak positively of their increased ability to listen with understanding to others.

Your reasons for becoming a client may be any of these suggested, or it may be something known only to you. Whatever the reason, counselling involves change. It can change not only your life, but your relationships with others. Maybe it is the prospect of change that holds you back, but change can be exciting and stimulating. Counselling is one way of helping you make positive changes in your life, rather than feel helpless to influence your future.

May your journey through counselling prove to be exciting, stimulating and fruitful, and may the experience prove to be beneficial not only to you but also other people whose lives you touch.

ANGELA WRITES

William and I had both worked as counsellors for many years when I came to a point in my life at which I needed someone to counsel me. Being a counsellor does not protect anyone from having problems or difficulties for which they need help, and I was fortunate to find in William a counsellor who not only shared my understanding and approach to people and their needs, but also had skills, warmth and sensitivity to my way of being.

After our work together as counsellor and client had been completed, I was delighted to accept William's invitation to collaborate on this book, the purpose of which is to demystify the process of counselling and make it accessible to you, the reader.

Our brief is to encompass the core experience of being a client, to enable you to gain maximum benefit from the process, and to help you work with your counsellor to develop awareness and essential life skills. Our training and work as counsellors over the years, our personal experience of receiving counselling, and our learning from our clients inform the text. It is not always easy to decide to enter counselling; it may feel like entering a maze to find or choose a counsellor, and it may be even more difficult to know what to expect from the experience.

If you are considering counselling we hope this book will address your hopes and fears, answer your queries and enable you to use your own resources to achieve your goals. Above all we hope you will gain an understanding of the most essential part of the process, namely the relationship between you, the client, and your counsellor.

William Stewart and Angela Martin

1

Deciding if You Want Counselling

*If I keep from meddling with people, they take care of
themselves,*
If I keep from commanding people, they behave themselves,
If I keep from preaching at people, they improve themselves,
If I keep from imposing on people, they become themselves.

M. Friedman[1]

The aim of this chapter is to help you decide if counselling is for
you. You may be experiencing some difficulty in your life, possibly a problematic relationship, or perhaps you have reached a
crossroad in your life and would like to talk through the options
with someone who is not involved. The counselling partnership
will help you focus on what you want and how to work towards
achieving your goal.

DEFINING COUNSELLING

There are many definitions of what counselling is. Simply, it is a
working relationship in which clients are helped to explore what is
happening in their lives, and through the relationship to work
towards living life with greater well-being which empowers them
to take control of the direction of their life.

Not every person who uses counselling skills is designated a
'counsellor'. We can distinguish two broad groups of people who
use counselling skills:

- people who are called counsellors, who engage in counselling
  as a distinct occupation

- and others who use counselling skills as part of their other skills.

Doctors and nurses are examples of professionals who use counselling skills as part of their repertoire of skills.

Making use of counselling

Counselling will help you make some sense out of confusion, choice from conflict and sense out of nonsense. Counselling will help you discover resources hitherto not recognised and helps you put those resources to work on your own behalf. Whatever the focus in counselling, it must always be on your needs, and any action taken must always be your decision.

You may use the counselling relationship to:

- deal with developmental issues
- address and resolve specific problems
- make decisions
- cope with crises
- develop personal insights and knowledge
- work through feelings of inner conflict
- improve relationships with others
- learn new life skills and techniques.

Counselling is entered into of your own free will and is a specific arrangement between you and the counsellor. In the majority of instances, you become a client to a full-time counsellor who has no other role.

WORKING WITH YOUR UNIQUE SELF

One of the fundamental principles of counselling is that of respect for, and acceptance of, the uniqueness of each person. Whoever you are, whatever your background, problems, life-style, status or behaviour, you will be respected and accepted. Of course there may be many similarities between what two people present to a counsellor, but the essence of the counselling relationship is that the counsellor responds to you as a unique person, and will not try to fit you into some predetermined mould or pattern.

Working with your counsellor in a partnership

In several places we refer to this point – that counselling is a partnership. It could be argued that the doctor/patient relationship is a partnership, but that is true only to a limited extent, for various reasons. The role of the doctor is to diagnose and then prescribe. The doctor has other functions, of course, and some doctors do listen very attentively to their patients, and some are excellent counsellors, but counselling is not their main function. It is also true that for the prescribed treatment to work you, the patient, have a vital part to play. You must have faith in the doctor and his diagnosis and you must be willing to accept the treatment prescribed.

Unlike medicine, diagnosing does not play an essential role in counselling. Diagnosis consists of observation, an essential facet of counselling, but it also implies examination by questions, applying preconceived principles and criteria, and a process of elimination. Successful treatment is dependent on accurate diagnosis, and cannot start until that process is completed. In most counselling approaches the word 'treatment' is not used and the process starts immediately, as counsellor and client begin to interact. Similarly, most counsellors will not concentrate on minute history-taking, preferring to build up the picture over time as the essential details are revealed.

Working in partnership towards insight

Partnership has an entirely different meaning from treatment, which is why it is an appropriate word to apply to counselling. First, partnership implies equality, a relationship of equals. You may wonder how this can apply to counselling, where the counsellor is a professional and you are not. While this is true, it is not the whole truth.

In a business partnership, say of three people, you may have an accounts person, a computer person and a front person. They all have different skills, yet they are equal partners. In hospitals there are teams, where each person – doctor, nurse, physiotherapist, occupational therapist – all contribute to the partnership. Just so in counselling.

While the counsellor has an important part to play, he or she would not be in that role if you, the client, were not there. The counsellor's role is to:

- listen

- take in what you say

- process it

• and then reflect what you have said, in such a way that your understanding is increased and you work towards greater insight to help you achieve whatever your goal is.

Your role is, in many ways, similar to that of the counsellor. If you do not listen, take in, reflect and process what the counsellor is saying, then the counselling process will grind to a halt. That is why counselling is a partnership.

ENHANCING YOUR SELF-ESTEEM THROUGH COUNSELLING

Many people who have difficulties – in whatever area of life, be it work or at a personal level – suffer from damaged **self-esteem**. Many different life experiences damage self-esteem. Quite often low self-esteem results from relationships at a young age, where parents and those in positions of authority continually undermine the developing child, often by comments that put the child down and reinforce the feeling of low worth. Children who grow up with a healthy self-esteem are often more able in later life to suffer the knocks of living. The counselling relationship will encourage you to repair damaged self-esteem for here, where you are free from judgement and criticism, you are able to start to respect yourself.

Sorting out confused feelings

If you are emotionally confused, counselling will help you make some sense out of confusion; choice from conflict and sense out of nonsense. Counselling will help you discover resources which you have hitherto not recognised, and help you put those resources to work for your benefit. The overall aim of counselling is an improvement in your well-being, in that you are more able to take control of the direction of your life. Whatever the focus in counselling, it must always be on your needs, and any action taken must always be your decision. If counselling is to be successful, the counsellor must depend, for the most part, on your own potential for growth.

Counselling is not a panacea

Counselling is not a cure for all of life's ills. Indeed many difficulties cannot be cured, but finding hidden resources can help to make the wheels of your life run more smoothly.

Some common myths about counselling

- Counselling is simply being a good listener.
- Counselling lasts for years.
- Counselling is only for rich people.
- Counsellors are only interested in sex.
- I have to tell the counsellor all my secrets.
- Counselling is only giving advice.
- If I go for counselling, I must be sick.
- Counselling is just being friendly.
- The counsellor will psychoanalyse me.
- Counselling will exploit my weaknesses.
- Counsellors are just well-meaning do-gooders.
- Counsellors are playing at being psychiatrists.
- Counsellors have to be perfect before they can help other people.
- Counsellors tell people what they should do.
- Counsellors solve other people's problems.
- Counselling will take responsibility away from me.

Some truths about counselling

- Counselling can help you unblock your feelings.
- Counselling can help you to understand yourself better.
- Counselling is a two-way process.
- Counselling can be brief or long-term.
- People of all types and ages go for counselling.
- Counselling can increase your self-confidence.
- Whatever your problem, counselling can help you deal with it.
- Counselling can help you take charge of your life.
- It takes courage to go for counselling.
- Counsellors also have difficulties in their lives.
- Your counsellor will not tell you what to do.
- Your strengths are important in counselling.
- Counselling can help you to build your self-esteem.
- Counselling can improve your relationships.
- Counselling can enable you to manage stress.
- Counselling will help you to set and achieve goals.
- Counselling can help you solve your own problems.

Fig. 1. Myths and truths about counselling.

The counsellor will not solve your problems. The counsellor is there to help clarify and facilitate, and assist you to find an acceptable solution to your own problems. Neither is the counsellor's goal to make you better adjusted to society. The counsellor is there for you, not as an agent of society which would have implications of conformity and compliance which most counsellors would certainly not agree to.

There are many professionals, such as probation officers, police officers, social services workers, who do use counselling skills and are agents of society. Theirs is a special relationship which holds respect for, and acceptance of, their client, yet at the same time they are of necessity operating within the constraints and requirements of authority.

IDENTIFYING WHY COUNSELLING IS NOT ADVICE-GIVING

Advice frequently means telling people what they should do or ought to do, and this has no place in counselling. The counsellor will help you look at what is *possible*, and will not tell you what you should do. That would be the counsellor *taking* control rather than you *gaining* control.

The counsellor who answers the question 'What would you advise me to do?' with 'What ideas have you had?' is helping you to realise that you have a part to play in seeking an answer. They help you take responsibility for finding a solution that feels right for you.

Advice is often appropriate in crises; at times when your thoughts and feelings seem stunned by the event. At times like these the counsellor will exercise greater caution than when you are fully responsive and responsible. Advice offered and accepted when in crisis, and then acted upon, could prove to be if not 'bad advice', not totally appropriate to meet your needs. When you are under **stress** you are vulnerable. For all of those reasons, counsellors are wary about responding to a request for advice.

However, it is sometimes very difficult not to offer advice. If you are stressed, for example, the counsellor may advise you on how to relax, and what steps to take to reduce stress levels. Even though the 'advice' might be 'good', the choice is always yours.

Offering reassurance is not counselling's role

Counsellors will try not to offer reassurance. Unwarranted, false reassurances are a violation of respect, for they are an attempt to diminish the problem in the eyes of the other person. The mere fact that the counsellor is taking time to help you explore the problem, and is creating a climate conducive to foster exploration, is adequate reassurance. The sort of reassurance that is empty and meaningless is 'It will all work out right, don't worry.' If you have been on the receiving end of this type of comment, when your world seems as if the bottom has dropped out of it, you will know the feelings of frustration they generate in you.

Unenlightened people attempt to relieve other people's anxiety by trying to prove to them that things are not as bad as they think. Inappropriate verbal reassurances stifle any further meaningful discussion, leaving you feeling not listened to. Counsellors know how essential it is that you experience the depths of your feelings in order to work through them towards understanding and insight.

Unwarranted reassurances often reflect people's inability to handle their own anxiety and frustration. Reassurances may be a refusal to acknowledge the reality of your feelings. If you perceive something as a mountain, then a mountain it is. Positive reassurance is conveyed indirectly through the counsellor's skills of active listening and responding, within a relationship in which you feel respected and accepted.

Exploring why counselling is not persuasion

Counselling is not persuading, prevailing upon, overcoming your resistance, wearing you down or 'bringing you to your senses'. Persuasion is in direct conflict with at least one principle of counselling, self-direction – your right to choose for yourself your course of action. If the counsellor were to persuade you to go a certain way, make a certain choice, there could be a very real danger of the whole affair backfiring in the face of the counsellor and resulting in further damage to your self-esteem.

This concept of self-direction, based on your freedom, is the touchstone of the non-directive approach to counselling but is present in most others. The basis of the principle is that:

- any pressure which is brought to bear on you will create or increase conflict and so hamper exploration.

We all know from our own experience, particularly with our parents or teachers, that any attempt to persuade us to adopt or pursue a certain course of action which may not tally with what we want, may cause certain things to happen!

Dealing with persuasion
If you have a high regard for, or are afraid of, the persuader, you may swallow your resentment and capitulate. If you are continually forced into this situation, although outwardly compliant a build-up of resentment is inevitable. The result is that the resentment will cause a rift in the relationship, or you may become so compliant that you are completely dominated and unable to exercise your own choice in anything.

Another course of action would be for you to outwardly comply then go your own way, surreptitiously. Yet another outcome of persuasion is that when you are persuaded against your will, you will do what was expected of you but half-heartedly. In this circumstance, failure is virtually predestined. There is of course the possibility that you may openly rebel. In such circumstances the persuader is likely to be heard saying plaintively, 'I just cannot understand why he is like that; after all I have tried to do for him.'

Exploring why the counsellor will not tell you what to do
All of the above applies equally in counselling. It is certainly true that you may wish to please your counsellor because you hold them in high regard, and you may think that your counsellor would want you to follow a particular course of action. Implicit in this is 'They are wiser, more experienced than I am, therefore they *must* know what is best for me.' However, the desired results may not necessarily follow.

If you are experiencing emotional conflict your reasoning powers are affected and you may agree to something which, in normal circumstances, you would reject. If this is so, it is not difficult to appreciate that when the conflict has passed, and your emotional balance is partially if not completely restored, you may then reject that to which you agreed earlier.

Direction is not generally accepted as part of counselling. Giving direction is another form of control, and counselling is to do with empowering *you* to take control. If your goal is to develop self-awareness and insight, then the counsellor will enable you to explore options, but the final choice is yours. In certain circumstances the counsellor might advise you, for example, to consult your GP, or possibly seek a more specialised counsellor, but the choice would still be yours.

Identifying why counselling is not exercising undue influence

Some people believe that successful counsellors are those who are able to suggest solutions to clients' problems in such a way that the clients feel they are their own. This is commonly called 'manipulation', behaviour from which most counsellors would recoil. However, situations are seldom clear cut. There is a fine line between legitimate influence and manipulation. Manipulation always carries with it some benefit to the manipulator. Influence is generally unconscious. In any case, suggesting solutions is not part of effective counselling. There is a difference between exploring alternatives and suggesting solutions and manipulation. Manipulation will always leave you feeling uncomfortable, used and angry.

Identifying why counselling is not manipulation
Counselling definitely *is not* manipulation, which is 'unfair influence'; something underhand, a plot, duplicity.

When one person *persuades* you to do or attempt something (even though it may be against your better judgement or wishes), it is usually done in such a way that you realise what is happening. The person who *manipulates* you to do what he or she wants does so subversively, not in the open, and (this is the essential difference) usually for some personal gain and not in your best interests.

- The dividing line between manipulation and seeking ways and means to resolve a problem may not always be easily seen, but the deciding factor must be *who benefits*? Is it you, or is it the other person?

An example of manipulation, taken from a training session, illustrates the point. Joe was passing through a difficult time with his girlfriend. The trainee counsellor, in the belief that it would be best for Joe to end the relationship, introduced a whole gamut of moral issues which made Joe feel so guilty that he said he would sever the relationship. This would have been inappropriate and would have left both Joe and the girl feeling resentful. That is manipulation.

Understanding why counselling is not psychoanalysis

Psychoanalysis is a therapy developed by Freud. Counsellors are not psychoanalysts, and counselling is not psychoanalysis. The principal difference between psychoanalysis and counselling is that psychoanalysis deals more, but not exclusively, with the unconscious and the past, while counselling deals more, but not exclusively with the conscious and the present – the here-and-now and the very recent past. Counselling cannot ignore the past, for it is the past which has made us the way we are now. It is inevitable that things from the past will pop through into the conscious present.

'More, but not exclusively' needs to be qualified. The counsellor cannot ignore the unconscious. The past and the present are bound together with cords that cannot be broken and it is inevitable that things from the past will pop through into the conscious present. When this happens the client will usually be aware of it. This flash of insight carries with it a certain excitement and anticipation of pleasure. It is like walking into a house which you have not visited for many years – it is vaguely familiar. Merely a smell, a picture, a sound, will bring back floods of forgotten memories and emotions.

When this happens, both you and the counsellor can be caught up in excitement as you feel that here at last is 'the' clue to the whole problem. However, both psychoanalysts and counsellors know that more exploration is needed.

Exploring the past

We do not want to give the impression that exploration of the past has no place in counselling or that probing is inappropriate and unnecessary. We have said that the past and the present are inseparable and if this is so then the one cannot be examined without some part of the other emerging; it is all a matter of degree and emphasis.

The past will show its influence quite clearly; and if dealt with when appropriate, will yield fruit. Too much emphasis on the past can detract from the present. If the counselling relationship helps you to learn to do your own exploring you will have acquired a valuable tool which you can put to good use in the future.

Solving your problems for yourself

The counsellor will enable you to look at problem-solving strategies, but cannot solve your problems. If the counsellor could do this, it would put you in an inferior position. You would become dependent. The aim is to help you explore what the problem is, then you and the counsellor work out how you might go about resolving the problem. However, some problems may never be solved, but you may learn strategies to manage them more effectively.

Neither does counselling remove your self-responsibility. In fact, the reverse is true. What has happened is that your coping powers have become temporarily 'frozen', and within the warmth of the counselling relationship they will become 'unfrozen' and mobilised, and you will feel strong enough to take action for yourself when counselling ends.

DECIDING IF COUNSELLING WOULD HELP YOU

Most people seek counselling because they are experiencing a problem in their lives which, however much they try, however much they think about it, they cannot seem to resolve. If you find that what started as a simple problem has grown to such an extent that it interferes with your sleep, appetite, relationships and work, then counselling might be helpful. You may approach your GP for help. He may offer medication, or suggest counselling; that would depend on the nature of the difficulty. For example, if you have been through a divorce, or break up of a relationship, suffered a bereavement, or lost your job, then psychological help through counselling might be more appropriate than medication. However, it is always as well to check with your GP if you do experience physical symptoms. People in counselling are not 'patients', unless they also happen to be in hospital. Being a patient has overtones of illness, and also of cure. Becoming a client does not imply illness, neither do counsellors speak of cure. On the contrary:

- counsellors work with your strengths, not your weaknesses.

Counselling might not be suitable for all problems. If there is an underlying medical problem, then the specialist help of your GP is the first approach. Almost all medical conditions may carry with them emotional difficulties, and it is then that the GP might consider referring you for counselling. For example, you may have suffered a miscarriage and feel anxious about further pregnancies; counselling will help you work through the anxiety. You may be struggling with a long-term illness, and find that the emotional burden is getting you down. Counselling will not be able to cure the condition, but exploring your feelings might help you live life with more peace.

Weighing up whether counselling is for you

You might feel that by going for counselling other people will label you as weak or sick. It is true, they might. And that might be the biggest hurdle to overcome; what other people think of us is a powerful weapon in helping us decide what to do. If you are considering going for counselling, then one question might help you to decide:

- Can I cope with this (my difficulty) on my own?

If the honest answer is no, then probably you do need to accept, in spite of what other people might think, that you need help.

There are many situations in life where seeking help from a counsellor will enable you to manage your life more effectively. Mental illness is seldom dealt with by counsellors, unless they are especially trained. More often, people seek counselling because something has temporarily upset their emotional balance, or they feel they are finding it difficult to cope.

You may have told yourself that you should be able to manage your own problems, steer your own ship. Deciding to go for counselling could be a sign of *strength*. Acknowledging that here is one time when you are not self-sufficient could be the first step on a new road towards more understanding of yourself. Reaching out and asking for support, therefore, is taking positive action to be in control of your life.

CASE STUDY

Mike accepts the challenge

Mike was in a particularly stressful job in the Army. He had split up with his girlfriend and was in debt. Everything piled up, and he took an overdose of paracetamol but gave a false name at the hospital so that the Army authorities would not be informed. On the advice of a friend he telephoned me. His challenge was to get his life under control again, rather than being controlled by events. Mike learned techniques to reduce his stress level, which then freed him to explore his feelings and his options. After seven sessions he had gained some skills to help him in the future and felt able to manage on his own.

CHOOSING A COUNSELLOR

The same degree of care should go into choosing a counsellor as choosing a doctor. Most people shop around before asking to go on a GP's list. Usually you will listen to what other people have to say before making up your mind. In the same way, you will normally ask opinions before you entrust your house to a builder, or your car to a mechanic, so why not be as particular when seeking a counsellor?

One of the difficulties is that some people are more reluctant to talk about the counselling they have received than about how efficient their mechanic is. Yet there is probably nothing more reliable than personal recommendation. I once bought an expensive piece of fitness equipment, but before I made the deal I asked the company if they could put me in touch with a customer. Naturally this raises issues of confidentiality, so they contacted a particular person who agreed that I telephone. Speaking to someone first-hand convinced me. There is no reason why a counsellor would not do this, for if another client agrees to talk to you then there is no breach of confidentiality.

If you cannot rely on personal recommendation, or referral by your GP, there are other sources such as the Citizen's Advice Bureau who will normally be able to provide a list of counselling agencies. The British Association for Counselling (BAC) (address in Useful Addresses) will provide a list of counsellors in your locality, though they will not recommend any one in particular; or look in the Counselling and Advice section in *Yellow Pages*. Another source of information would be your local college, if they run counselling courses as many of them now do.

All that can be quite daunting, especially if you are feeling under pressure or in the middle of a crisis. It's a bit like discovering a broken tank in the loft and water is pouring down the stairs – you would ring an emergency plumber, any plumber, for this is a real emergency. Yet most householders would have made a note of a reliable plumber on whom they could call, for the time to think about qualifications, reliability, standards and so on is not when water is pouring out of every crack.

There the simile ends. Whatever your particular crisis, does it warrant taking the first counsellor you come across in *Yellow Pages*? Is there any situation you can imagine that would not wait a day or so to enable you to find a counsellor whom you feel would meet your requirements?

If you make contact by telephone (and mostly this is how it happens), this is the sort of information you need in order to make an informed choice.

Qualifications

While qualifications are no guarantee of quality, the fact that a person does have appropriate qualifications is an indication of having achieved a certain standard in a chosen subject.

Training

There are various routes. Some people are professionals in their own right, such as doctors, nurses, clergymen, psychologists, who then go on to further training in counselling. This may be at a college or university, or through one of the counselling agencies such as Relate or Cruse. Other people undertake a college-based training, which involves both theory and practice. For all counsellors there is an obligation to continue their development through further training, supervision and support. The British Association for Counselling (BAC) Code of Ethics (B2.3.2) reads, 'Counsellors should have received adequate basic training before commencing counselling, and should maintain ongoing professional development.'

It is a requirement of most counselling training that the student undertakes personal counselling. No training can be a substitute for personal counselling, for it is this which gives substance to what takes place in the classroom. It is personal counselling which further develops self-awareness. Before people can be accredited by BAC they must have a set number of hours of personal counselling.

Throughout a counsellor's professional life it may be necessary to undergo further counselling. Counsellors are not immune to crises and traumas, and although they may be very experienced and can still work with their clients, they may again need to become clients themselves to work through a particular difficult time in their lives. Having been a client gives the counsellor first-hand experience of what the counsellor-client relationship means.

Experience
For example the type of jobs held, or the length of time as a counsellor, is an indication of reliability.

Accreditation
The British Association for Counselling (BAC) was formed as a voluntary association and charity in 1977 and is now a registered company. It has its roots in the Standing Conference for the Advancement of Counselling, formed in the late 1960s. Membership is individual or organisational. There are various divisions within BAC. The aims are to raise the standards of counselling and to promote understanding of it. Counsellors can become accredited members, and although compulsory accreditation and registration has been proposed, it is not yet mandatory. You can get information about counsellors in your area who are BAC members from BAC headquarters. If you have a complaint against your counsellor you may approach BAC, or if the counsellor is not a BAC member the Citizen's Advice Bureau will advise you how to lodge a complaint. Accreditation is one way of ensuring that your counsellor has been accepted by a recognised body, though, as with any qualification, this is no guarantee that you and the counsellor will hit it off.

Particular approaches
This subject will be developed later, but for now it would be useful to introduce five main approaches which counsellors use.

- In the psychodynamic, which is based on psychoanalysis, the counsellor points to the underlying dynamics, helping clients to achieve insight into their drives which influence behaviour.

- For behaviour therapists the focus is on changing behaviour. The basic premise is that all behaviour is learnt, and that well-being can be enhanced by appropriate change in behaviour.

- Similarly, cognitive therapists work to the premise that all behaviour is influenced by what we think. Feelings of low self-worth, for example, are triggered by negative thoughts.

- Carl Rogers developed the person-centred approach where, rather than trying to fit the client into some predetermined model, the idea is to work with what the client says and feels. The counsellor strives to understand what something means to the client, rather than fitting it into some psychological theory.

- Many counsellors use an integrated or eclectic approach, using many techniques from different theories, according to the needs of the client at a specific moment.

Supervision

All counsellors need to receive regular supervision from another counsellor or counsellors. The benefits of supervision are support, teaching and integrating theory and practice, together with assessment and maintenance of standards of work, professional values and ethics.

Fees

Counsellors generally charge a fee, and may operate a sliding scale. If you really cannot afford the full fee, it is important that you discuss it, rather than the fee becoming a source of worry and possible resentment to you. It is generally accepted that free

Pointers	Comments
Qualifications	
Training	
Experience	
Accreditation	
Approach(es)	
Supervision	
Fees	
General feel	
Overall evaluation	

Fig. 2. Evaluating potential counsellors.

counselling can leave you feeling patronised, and the recipient of charity, and the counsellor may feel exploited. Some GP practices fund counselling for the patients, and some churches and voluntary organisations provide free counselling.

General 'feel'.
Finally, try to avoid being pushed into making an instant decision about going for counselling. Absorb and evaluate the information you have gleaned from your chat with the counsellor or from a number of counsellors. Say you will ring back to make an appointment, if you feel hesitant. You could use the table in Figure 2 to help with your search for a counsellor.

There are five main pointers which might help you to make a decision as to which counsellor is for you.

Tone of voice
Speaking at the other end of a telephone means that you cannot read the body language, but how comfortable did you feel talking to the counsellor? Did you feel you had the counsellor's time, or did you feel hurried? However, don't expect to be counselled over the telephone.

Warmth
What words did the counsellor use that conveyed warmth? Did you feel the counsellor was understanding you?

Openness
How open was the counsellor in replying to your questions?

Information
Did you get all the information you wanted? How readily was this information provided?

Listening
Did the counsellor demonstrate listening skills?

CASE STUDIES

Joan is referred by her GP
I received a letter from one of the local doctors, asking if I would be willing to see a patient of his, Joan. She had been through an

exploratory abdominal operation just over a year ago, and since then she had lost her zest for life. I agreed to see Joan, if she would telephone me to make an appointment.

This was a straightforward referral, and personal recommendation from a doctor who had referred clients to me before. Joan did not 'shop around'. She was happy with her GP's choice.

Mark asks questions

Unlike Joan, Mark came through *Yellow Pages*. He was suffering from long-term stress, which was affecting his work in advertising. One of the factors was a recent acrimonious divorce. I was the third counsellor he had telephoned. One of the questions he asked was, 'How do you manage your own stress?' This seemed a perfectly sensible question to ask, so I told him some of the things I did to prevent the build-up of stress. Mark did become a client, and one of the first things he said was, 'What helped me make up my mind was your honesty. I got the impression that you knew what you were talking about.'

SUMMARY

1. In this chapter we looked at something of what counselling is and is not. Most of what was discussed will be developed in later chapters, but what emerges here is that counselling is a purposeful relationship with you, the client, at the centre. It is you who decides the direction, the focus and what to explore. The counsellor acts as a facilitator. This means that by using certain counselling skills the counsellor will help you make sense of out what seems nonsense, so that you can move forward towards your chosen goal.

2. Counselling brings out your hidden resources, to help you make choices and decisions. Thus counselling empowers. It helps you make changes that you feel will benefit you. The counselling relationship is a springboard for positive action.

3. Counselling is not only about helping you resolve problems; it is also about personal development. As you gain insight into your inner self, you will find that you have more understanding of yourself and other people. However, counselling is not some miracle cure and will not solve all your problems. Some

situations in life cannot be resolved, but developing your resources can help you manage difficult situations more easily.

4. Before you commit yourself to a counselling relationship, find out as much as you can about a particular counsellor or counsellors, then make your choice. If you are suffering from a grief reaction, then an appropriate counsellor is one who works in this area. If you are in the grip of an addiction, then you need to check out if a particular counsellor takes this type of work. If you are suffering from stress, then seek a counsellor who does stress work. These are vital questions to be asking in your search for a counsellor. This preliminary work demonstrates to you and the counsellor that you intend that counselling will be a partnership.

2

Assessing Special Considerations

This chapter helps you explore any special considerations you may have in choosing a particular counsellor. For example, you might want to choose a counsellor of the same sex, similar age, religion and so on. Knowing your reasons for the choices you make will help you to get the most from the counselling, because you will feel more in control. If you have special needs, knowing the questions to ask stresses the idea of partnership.

Many counsellors work with a wide range of different clients, and do not specialise; they could be termed 'generic' counsellors. Some, however, do specialise and very often these are the people to whom other counsellors will refer clients.

The parallel between a GP and a specialist is obvious. If you think of the generic counsellor as the GP, then the patient about whom the doctor has doubts will refer to a specialist in, say, heart disease or orthopaedics. This the choice of counsellor may well be guided by the particular reason you seek counselling. This theme will be explored in Chapter 6, where we look at some particular life situations. For now, however, there are some issues which may influence your choice of counsellor.

EXPLORING WHETHER AGE DIFFERENCE INFLUENCES YOUR CHOICE

Age seldom presents difficulties in counselling. Unlike for example nursing, where the students are predominantly young, counsellors do tend to be older.

Many people have come into counselling after having trained in other areas, such as medicine, psychology, nursing, the ministry, school teaching, or having raised a family. They now feel able to embark on a second or third career.

Many people become counsellors having been through the experience themselves, and this is a useful preparation for there is nothing like having been on the receiving end of something to increase awareness. Being a patient in my childhood, with life-threatening diphtheria, led me into becoming a nurse. A colleague who had suffered a traumatic divorce, and received counselling, in turn became a counsellor.

It does seem that life experience is an essential element in counselling, but age does not necessarily equate with experience, ability or understanding. Many of the qualities essential in the counsellor do not develop simply by age or maturity. The essence of these qualities are undoubtedly there within the person. If they were not, it is questionable if any amount of training would result in their growth.

Counselling training can only work with what is there.

Assessing how age affects a counsellor's work

There is a myth that age necessarily equates with wisdom. To a degree that is true, but it is no guarantee. One view is that young people do not have the necessary skills and experience to be effective counsellors. Some social work students of the course I was on were young, most of them coming straight from first degree courses, and I know (because some of the students told me) that a few of their clients thought them too young to really know what they were talking about, to understand what they were going through.

To put this into perspective, not all that happens in life is beneficial or positive. In the process of getting older we all, without exception, learn to put up barriers to shield us from getting hurt. Thus the older person, although mature and maybe with greater experience of life, has more to work through, more baggage to get rid of, more defences to get behind, before being in the position to help you, the client, explore your particular difficulty. So both youth or age have advantages and disadvantages.

Choosing an older counsellor

If the counsellor's age is a question mark for you, then ask yourself why. Do you find it more comfortable to be with someone of your own age, older or younger? If you get on better with older people, does that have echoes of your own relationship with your parents? Is there a part of you that needs to be in a relationship with an older person, for that creates a sense of security? That could have implications of wanting to be controlled, of wanting to be told what to do. If it is this, then such feelings could lead to you rebelling against the counsellor, rather than working with them in a partnership of equals.

Choosing a younger counsellor

If having a counsellor who is younger than you is important, why? This could mean that you want to be in a position of authority. This is the reverse of the previous position, and you could wish to tell the counsellor what to do, or to be able to impose your will on the relationship. If paraphrased it could be something like, 'I have more experience than you, so don't tell me what to do.'

Counsellors will rarely tell you what to do. Telling another person what to do, giving direction is, in counselling terms, called control. Direction is not generally accepted as part of counselling. Counselling is to do with empowering *you* to take control. If your goal is to develop self-awareness and insight, then the counsellor will enable you to explore options, but the final choice is yours. In certain circumstances the counsellor might advise you, for example, to consult your GP, but the choice would still be yours.

If you are doubtful about a particular counsellor on account of the counsellor being younger than you, then perhaps this is just part of a wider issue of how you relate to other people. Counselling could be one way, then, of helping you resolve that specific relationship problem.

Choosing a counsellor of your own age

If you search for a counsellor of about your own age, and if this is a major factor, then it is possible that friendship is an important aspect of the counselling relationship for you. While counsellors are friendly, counselling is not friendship, and counsellors will respect the difference. Not becoming friends does not mean that the counsellor does not like you, but counselling exists for a specific purpose and for the relationship to work it has to be kept at a professional level.

Even when the counselling relationship ends, it is often difficult to enter into friendship; it is as if the disclosures get in the way. Having been counsellor and client it is often difficult to lose that relationship. You might like to discuss with your counsellor the possible situation that you bump into each other in, say, the supermarket. How should both of you react?

EXPLORING WHY THE COUNSELLOR'S GENDER MIGHT BE RELEVANT

Just as some people prefer to have a doctor of the same gender, so in counselling. You might be more comfortable discussing intimate details with a counsellor of your own sex. However, you might find an opposite-sex counsellor is able to present a different view, or frame or reference, so that you can see something in a new light.

If, however, what you want to discuss is not of an intimate nature, and you still prefer a same-sex counsellor, then as with age ask yourself why. Counselling is:

- intimate in its sharing and disclosure, and this might give you a clue

- intimate because it is sharing your thoughts, feelings, desires, goals, successes and failures, and life experiences with another person, possibly things you do not share easily with your spouse or partner.

Perhaps intimacy is more comfortable with people of the same sex because of previous life experiences. The relationship one has with one's father or mother, or other principal carer, can influence our choice of with whom we share intimate details of our life. If the relationship with one or other of your parents was not close, then that might be a reason for choosing a counsellor of the different sex. On the other hand, there may be something deep within which you cannot explain which pushes you into choosing a counsellor of the same sex as the parent with whom you did not have a close relationship.

Try to express your doubts and reservations with your chosen counsellor, for just expressing how you feel could be a significant step in you working towards greater self-awareness.

CASE STUDY

In sessions with William June explores her childhood abuse

June suffered 14 years of physical abuse in a series of orphanages. This resulted in her later taking drugs and suffering from depression. In her mid-40s she chose to come to me to explore her feelings about those early years, with particular reference to her feelings about her mother, with whom she was experiencing an ambivalent relationship. Quite early on June disclosed that although she had had several relationships with men, she could never allow herself to have intercourse.

Over the course of many months we explored her feelings about her early years, and she gained a degree of insight and healing. On several occasions she mentioned the subject of sex, but it was clear that I was not the person she wanted to explore that with. Finally June agreed that I refer her to a female counsellor who specialised in sexual dysfunction. Although I had offered this early on in the relationship, it seemed that June had much other exploratory work to do before she could take the step of consulting another counsellor.

'Why did you choose me?' I asked. 'I've never got on too well with men, and I thought being in a professional relationship with a man would help me to understand different parts of myself.' This was one aspect. Another was that June did not get on well with women, particularly women in authority. We explored that theme many times, and June was able to become more assertive with women at work.

This short case study shows that for June there were two linked reasons for her choosing me as her counsellor. She had been recommended by a colleague of mine because 'I would be non-threatening.' June experienced a safe relationship with a man in which she could disclose intimate feelings and experiences, and who was able to help her look at her relationship with women, particularly the relationship with her mother. This prepared the way for June, when she was ready, to continue working with a female counsellor, exploring the more intimate details of sexual dysfunction.

EXPLORING HOW CULTURE MIGHT INFLUENCE YOUR CHOICE

This section is not a discussion about culture from a sociological point of view, but only as the various parts of culture might influence counselling.

Usually when we think of culture we mean people from different countries, different ethnic groups, but culture is broader than that. If you travel from Land's End to John O' Groats, how many counties will you pass through? Each has its different culture.

Language

Language is a fascinating subject, for by it we communicate our thoughts, feelings, ideas, values and many of the other important aspects of who we are. In our journey from one end of Britain to the other we would encounter subtle, but quite distinct, different uses of language.

If such misunderstanding may arise amongst people who speak the same language, what about if your first language is not English? What if the counsellor is of a different ethnic group and whose first language is not English? What difficulties could there be in either instance?

A personal anecdote illustrates how misunderstanding might arise. In my early 20s I lived in Sussex and worked for a Yorkshire farmer. One cold winter morning I was cutting and baling hay. This required deft knot-tying of twine. I was fumbling with the knots. 'Eh, lad, ye're hands be soft,' the farmer said. My pride was pricked. 'They're not soft,' I retorted, highly indignant. 'Nay, I know that,' he replied with a wide grin, 'don't take on so. In Yorkshire soft hands are cold.'

Words carry different meanings, as we have already seen in my own anecdote. That had its amusing side; but what about the deeper exploration of your feelings? You know what you want to say, but interpretation might not be so simple.

This difficulty is similar to two people listening to a piece of music. One may hear only the melody; the other hears all the notes of both melody and harmony. If you are of a different ethnic culture, the way you respond would be moderated by the length of time you have spent in this culture. If you are second, third or fourth generation residents of this country then you and your counsellor will probably find yourselves on the same wavelength.

CASE STUDY

Mavis doesn't understand

When I was a lecturer of counselling in a college of nursing, one group consisted largely of students from overseas. They all spoke English, but for many English was not their first language. They coped very well, in spite of the fact that many of them had never resided in England. One student in particular, Mavis, well-qualified in her own country, experienced great difficulty in group discussions. She appeared slow and at times looked quite distressed. There was no doubt that Mavis was suffering from culture shock, but there seemed to be more.

In one of the group sessions, when the group had been in training about one year, I said that people for whom English is not their first language often have to translate what they have heard into their own language and then retranslate into English before replying. This means that certain important points might be lost or become fuzzed. I wondered if this was how any of them found the group sessions.

The look of relief on Mavis's face was profound, as one and another of the group said this was exactly how it was for them. Mavis was the most articulate. Although she had received a super previous training, it was by English-speaking Africans and often carried out in their own language.

Another factor was that Mavis was not accustomed to discussion; almost all of her previous education had been the traditional 'talk and chalk'. As a result of the discussion we had, Mavis felt supported and understood. I and the other group members learnt to give much more time to one another, rather than expecting an instant response.

This might be something you have to consider when seeking a counsellor. Can you find one of your own ethnic group? Someone from your own culture has an instinctive awareness of what something means, whereas a counsellor from a different culture has to find out. This can be a rewarding experience for both you and the counsellor; for you, it means possibly delving into your own cultural history to find out why you do things the way you do, say the things that you do. For the counsellor, working with people from different cultures means raising awareness and words take on entirely different meanings.

Finding a counsellor of the same or similar culture might not be possible. If not, try to use the experience in a positive way. Taking Mavis as an example, tell the counsellor that that was not what you meant, or that you don't understand what the counsellor means. Let what you say convey what you mean. This is partnership in action.

Question your insight and self-awareness on culture

1. If you are female of a different culture from your counsellor, who is male, what feelings are generated within you?
2. Are you able to engage in a partnership relationship, or are there feelings that get in the way?

3. Do you find yourself engaged in a battle for dominance? If so, how much does this relate to your culture?
4. Is your culture male-dominated?
5. If you are male, of a different culture from your counsellor who is female, what feelings do you have about her?
6 How are women related to in your own culture?
7. In both instances – male or female – what influence did religion have on the development of attitudes towards females or towards males in your own culture?

EXPLORING HOW FAITH MIGHT INFLUENCE YOUR CHOICE

As with different cultures, counselling clients from different faiths can present difficulties, and it would be improper to suggest otherwise. Yet being of different faiths, or no faith at all, need not be any different than being counselled by someone of a different sex or age. Difference does not automatically mean lack of understanding. But your counsellor will need to take your beliefs into account, for they are an essential part of you.

I speak only for myself here, but I have been privileged to be the counsellor for atheists, humanists, Muslims, Hindu and Christians. And it is my experience that rather than one's faith (the client's and mine) getting in the way, the relationship has been enhanced by the greater understanding reached, even though faith may not have been discussed very much.

CASE STUDY

Ali mourns his father

Ali was a school teacher, a Hindu and married to a Hindu. He had been away from his homeland for many years and had done well in England. He came for personal therapy as part of the self-development requirements of his counselling training. We had developed a trusting relationship over several months, when he brought news that his father had died.

A rift in the family resulted in Ali not being told of his father's death until after his father had been cremated. The basic belief in Hindu religion is the cremated body returns to its elements of fire, water, air and earth, and is thus reunited with God. The eldest son lights the funeral pyre, while mantras and sacred texts are recited by the priest. Then follows a period of ritual where gifts of food are left for the soul of the departed. When this period is over, the bones of the deceased may be buried. Hindus believe in reincarnation (transmigration) which is the rebirth of the soul in one or more successive existences, which may be human, animal or, in some instances, vegetable.

Although not the eldest son, Ali was thrown in a deep depression of sadness and guilt that he had not been there to say goodbye to his father. Only as I explored with him the importance of that ceremony did I appreciate his feelings of betrayal and desertion. Viewing all this from his frame of reference was enlightening for me, and explaining it helped Ali to start to come out of his depression.

This would not be the place to discuss all the religions and how the faith of the counsellor might conflict with yours; what does seem more helpful is to show how it is possible to transcend particular faiths to arrive at one way in which you and your counsellor could stand on common ground.

UNDERSTANDING YOURSELF AND YOUR PAST

If you have thought about going for counselling, or are engaged in it, you will probably be aware of the suffering that comes from being stuck in your past, although that awareness may be hazy.

We are all influenced by our past, and for each of us there is a constant interaction between the three dimensions that make up the unique self. These three dimensions are:

- self

- society

- and beliefs.

There is constant interaction between all three dimensions; each working for harmony, yet producing various tensions.

What questions could you ask which would help you to understand yourself from each of the three standpoints of self, society and beliefs?

Considering self

- What do I think and feel about myself?

- What is my level of self-esteem?

- How do I relate to myself?

- Am I comfortable with myself and with others?

- What are my relationships with others like?

Considering society

- How do I relate to society and what do I think of my place in it?

- What are my relationships with various significant sections of society: parents, siblings, friends?

- What are my views about society?

- What are my views about work?

- Do I fit easily with society, or am I uncomfortable in it?

- Do I feel more at ease with certain groups in society than with others? If so, why?

Considering beliefs

- What are my views of God?

- What is my relationship to God?

- What are the foundations of my beliefs?

- How do my beliefs relate to self and society?

- How do I answer the questions if I do not believe in God?

- What is it that motivates me to higher things?

Identifying tensions

It may be helpful to see these three standpoints as different sides of a triangle. Fill in the boxes in Figure 3 with words or phrases representing your own unique unfluences. From each of the three boxes, take one thing at a time and contrast and compare it with those from the others, and see what tensions you can identify. Identifying tensions in this way means that you have some constructive ideas to discuss with your counsellor. You might find it helpful now to list the various tensions you identified.

Self

Society

Beliefs, Faith and Culture

The overall task of the unique you is to hold these three forces in tension. Fill in the boxes with words or phrases representing your own unique influences. See what tensions you can identify.

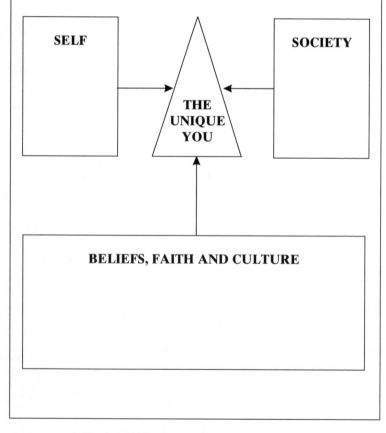

Fig. 3. Understanding your unique life story.

Example of Anne working with the model

Anne says she has a strong belief in God, yet she is also contemplating having an abortion because she is unmarried. What tensions might there be between **belief** and **self** and, possibly, **society**?

To continue this, Anne may believe that society sees her as being independent and responsible. To be an unmarried mother may remove some of that independence. To have an illegitimate child may not fit easily with her belief about morality.

Analysing the information from three different standpoints, then putting them all together, helps you to be aware of the tensions. Having once become aware, choice often becomes easier.

Understanding choices and changes

It will be helpful for both you and your counsellor if you have an idea of the changes you would like to make.

- In a few paragraphs summarise the influences on you and list what you would choose to change.

- Keep in mind that you are a product of what you inherited and past experiences, all of which influence you as you are now. By examining yourself and your environment calmly and thoroughly you can achieve a grasp of your alternatives and take action to create the life you want.

This will mean you are more able to relate the significant parts to your counsellor. Again, this demonstrates to both of you that you are active in the process and not merely a sleeping partner, waiting for the counsellor to initiate and do all the work.

CONSIDERING PRACTICAL DIFFICULTIES

Disability

People who have a disability may need counselling for the same reasons as any other person, or they may benefit from help in coming to terms with particular emotional difficulties resulting from their disability.

Rather than attempt to deal with the whole gamut of possible illnesses and conditions which can result in disability, we will concentrate on some of the difficulties which you, if you are disabled, might need to alert your counsellor to. Some of the factors to be considered are, difficulties of:

- speech

- sight

- hearing

- mobility

- concentration

- illness which makes travelling difficult.

If the counsellor is aware of the exact nature of your disability, then he or she can make arrangements. For example, having a ramp in place is an obvious solution if you are in a wheelchair or making sure that obstacles are removed from your path if you have difficulties with your sight.

Dependants

Other difficulties may arise if you have dependants whom you cannot leave, and this would naturally restrict contact. Although this situation is not strictly speaking a disability, it can so hamper you that it does have that effect. Tell your counsellor the circumstances and try to work out some compromise.

Fees

If you cannot afford the counsellor's charge, try not to let this stop you seeking or continuing counselling. Even a small reduction could help. If money is tight, and if travelling to the counsellor is expensive, some but not all counsellors arrange home visits, so that might be something to suggest to them.

Time

Time is another consideration for many people. Some counsellors only work 'office' hours, many have clients in the evenings. If you work, daytime sessions might be difficult for you. Again, do mention your particular difficulties. For example, Jeff worked away and could only come to see me at 8 in the mornings; that suited me, though it would not suit every counsellor.

Children

What do you do if you have young children to look after? Do you leave them with someone or bring them with you? Trying to carry on an intimate conversation with children present is almost impossible. Part of your willingness to become engaged in counselling would almost certainly involve finding someone to look after the children.

Other difficulties

Finally, there may be some difficulties that have not been discussed here, but take courage and present them to the counsellor. If the counsellor does not know that you cannot sit still for more than ten minutes, and that you have to get up and walk around, he or she will never know unless you say. The counsellor may pick up your restlessness and attribute it to something else. To reiterate, counselling is a partnership of mutual trust and respect, and a component of both of these is openness. One of the factors in your self-development might be overcoming the fear of being a nuisance. The counsellor would rather know than guess.

Your decision to become engaged in counselling should not be made lightly. Apart from the obvious consideration of money, counselling can work out expensive, though immensely satisfying and productive. Long-term counselling makes demands on your commitment, time, mental and emotional energy.

- The process started in the counselling session does not stop when you close the door behind you; you will find that you continue the exploration in the hours away from the counsellor.

- Insights will come to you at the oddest moments, triggered off by a chance remark, or a fleeting memory or a dream.

This is the excitement of counselling, and once again demonstrates that you are involved in the process. Nothing will give the counsellor more encouragement (and counsellors do need encouragement) than for you to say, 'I had this tremendous flash of insight, let me tell you.'

Recognising the journey ahead

On the other hand, being realistic, counselling is hard work! You may travel the road a long time before you achieve momentous insight. Yet from our experience, most clients feel more able to cope with life within a short time, even though some of the more dramatic changes take much longer. Counselling, for you the client, is a learning process and like all learning it takes place little by little.

SUMMARY

1. Counselling is a partnership. The counsellor will not tell you what to do nor solve your problems for you. They will enable you to look at problem-solving strategies, but if they could solve your problems it would put you in an inferior position. You would become dependent. The aim is to help you explore what the problem is, then together you work out how you might go about resolving it. Some problems may never be solved, but you may learn strategies to manage them more effectively.

2. The counsellor will not take responsibility away from you. In fact, the reverse is true. Your coping powers have become temporarily 'frozen', and within the warmth of the counselling relationship they will become 'unfrozen' and mobilised and you will feel strong enough to take action for yourself when counselling ends.

3. The counsellor is a facilitator who helps you to help yourself. They do this by exploring your situation with particular reference to your feelings, and from that exploration you will develop insights to enable you to take charge of your own life. You will develop skills and strategies to help you manage your life more effectively.

4. Various important considerations might influence your choice of counsellor – age, sex, culture, religion, faith, understanding yourself and your past. There may also be some practical difficulties in being a client.

3

Looking for Counsellor Qualities

By acceptance I mean a warm regard for him as a person of unconditional self-worth of value no matter what his condition, his behaviour or his feelings. It means a respect and liking for him as a separate person, a willingness to express his own feelings in his own way. It means an acceptance of and a regard for his attitudes of the moment, no matter how negative or positive, no matter how much they may contradict other attitudes he has held in the past.

Carl Rogers[2]

In this chapter we highlight certain qualities to look for in a counsellor. Although some of these qualities might not be evident in the initial contact, they are important. Not only do you need to be confident in the skills of your counsellor, in order to get the most out of the process you also need to feel safe, understood, valued and respected. How you feel with your counsellor is crucial to the development of the counselling relationship.

CASE STUDY

Sandra starts to feel safe

Sandra, who had never been for counselling before, had been referred by a friend because she was not coping well since the death of her mother several months previously. We had made contact by telephone. This is an extract taken from her journal.

'When Anne suggested I go for counselling I felt quite frightened. I've always been an independent person and it's usually other people who come to me for help, not the other way round. I also felt angry with Anne, for she had seen beneath my façade of cheerfulness. Anyway, having plucked up courage – and it took several days – I rang William. I'm not sure what I expected, probably a telephone interrogation, or something like that, but that's not how it was at all. I said something quite silly, like, "I've lost my mum and I'm not coping well." He said, "Your mum's died and now you feel your world has crashed around you." That was enough to start me crying. I was so embarrassed, but he just waited and said, "I'm still here." I've often said that my counselling started then, at that very moment. I knew we had made real contact. I mean, if someone at the other end of the line can pick up my feelings like that, then face to face must be better.

William sent me a very nice letter, outlining what we had talked about on the phone, which included his fee and directions how to get to him. I arrived feeling apprehensive. I had read what some other people had said about counselling, and some of it was not complimentary. Halfway there in the car I almost chickened out and wanted to turn round, but something kept me going, and I'm glad I did.'

FEELING SAFE

Sandra has expressed what many people feel as they think about counselling. Counselling will only be fruitful if you feel safe. Apprehension is normal. Even counsellors who have had many hours of personal therapy often still experience initial apprehension when once again they feel the need for more therapy.

There are several possible explanations for this. One is that the person has thought everything was all right, but now discovers that further exploration is necessary, and further exploration reawakens the feelings of the first time. But more than that; exploration always has the potential for growth and change, and change is not always comfortable.

Just how does the counsellor help a client feel safe? Sandra indicates that the process has already started, in the initial contact. First impressions are important. For example, did the counsellor seem businesslike? Was there evidence of respect? At the same time, was there:

- empathy
- genuineness
- warmth
- acceptance
- regard?

These are the 'core conditions' which Carl Rogers speaks of as being essential in counselling. Although Rogers was speaking specifically of person-centred counselling, to some degree they are present in whatever approach is used. Let's discuss these core conditions.

EXPLORING EMPATHY

Empathy is a word much used in counselling. It is sometimes confused with sympathy and with pity but it is not the same. A counsellor would have to feel sympathetic, but sympathy is generally regarded as being unhelpful, mainly because it does little to help.

Longman's dictionary defines empathy as:

1. The capacity for imaginatively sharing in another's feelings or ideas.
2. A method or technique in the appreciation of a work of art involving the imaginative recreation of a mood, feeling, or emotional state suggested by the work of art in order to understand it better.

Although sympathy and empathy both mean 'sharing in another's feelings' sympathy lays emphasis on the idea of compassion for distress, while empathy involves imaginative identification with the other person.

Kaplan defines empathy as:

A capacity for one individual to put him or herself into the psychological frame of reference of someone else and thereby understand his or her thinking, feeling of behaviour.

This second definition is more precise when applied to psychological therapies such as counselling.

Our own definition of empathy in action is the ability of the counsellor to step into the inner world of the client and to step out of it again, yet to retain his or her identity without becoming the client. It means the counsellor tries to understand your thoughts, feelings, behaviours and personal meanings from your frame of reference. For empathy to mean anything, the counsellor has to respond in such a way that you feel that understanding has been reached, or is being striven for. Empathy is not a state that one reaches, nor a qualification that one is awarded. It is a transient thing. We can move in to it and lose it again very quickly. It means getting alongside and staying there for as long as possible and in such a way that you, the client, feel in close companionship.

You will feel when you and your counsellor are in empathy. If empathy means the counsellor stepping gently into your inner world, and seeing things from your frame of reference, trying to look at the world through your eyes, then this means that you must allow the counsellor in. If you put up barriers, either deliberately or unconsciously, empathy will be broken. The counsellor will feel this, and probably reflect it, thus demonstrating that he or she is still trying to understand what it feels like for you. Empathy, then, is a two-way process.

Understanding frames of reference

Before continuing the discussion of empathy, it would be useful to clarify what is meant by 'frame of reference'. The frame of reference is what makes each of us a unique person. Various factors of life have created this unique individual, including beliefs, thoughts, memories, experiences, feelings, meanings, perceptions, character, personality, sensations, behaviours, values, education, and culture. Although other people share all of these, the way they incorporate them into their frame of reference will be different. We have all been through the education system, but the impact that experience had is different for everybody. We have all had parents, but our relationship with them is different and unique. Even children within the same family experience their parents differently. Thus your frame of reference is unique to you.

In *Learning to Counsel* (Jan Sutton and William Stewart) frames of reference are seen as a two-part concept; the internal and the external. The internal frame of reference is your inner world; the external frame of reference is the inner world of the counsellor. When the counsellor is in empathy with you, there is movement from the external frame of reference. Then the counsellor 'knows' what something means to you. If the counsellor remains in the external frame of reference, you are being looked at through their meanings, not through your own eyes. Seeing things from the external frame of reference does not lead to understanding of what something means to you. When the counsellor views you and your behaviour through your eyes, it makes more sense.

Bridging the frames of reference

Empathy is the bridge which enables the counsellor to step into your frame of reference. But an essential element in empathy is for the counsellor to be able to step back into his or her own world, or frame of reference. If they were to become too immersed in *your* inner world, then objectivity would be lost, and the counsellor, effectively, would temporarily have become you and would experience all your feelings. This would not be productive. In order for constructive work to be done the counsellor, having glimpsed what something means to you, has to cross the bridge and come back into his or her own frame of reference. For it is from there that the counsellor is able to reflect *your* feelings and engage in the next stages of exploration.

Understanding sympathy

- Sympathy means becoming immersed in the other person's feelings.

- Empathy means the counsellor trying to understand your thoughts, feelings and behaviours but still remaining outside of them and trying to communicate to you an awareness of those feelings.

The principal of sympathy is that the feeling of one person is likely to cause similar feelings in another. In this sense, person B has become 'infected' with the feeling of person A. For example, panic, mob frenzy, weeping and wailing, religious ecstasy are all examples of sympathetic vibrations, though such feelings are generally short-lived; when the stimulus is removed, people will return to their normal emotional state.

At a different level, we may become more deeply involved with the other person's feelings, as if the chord which is struck makes more impact on us; this is probably sympathy proper. For example, we will be more likely to respond differently and with more sympathy to one of our children in distress than to observing someone else's child crying, or to watching a TV programme. We may feel sympathy towards certain groups in society, yet at the same time have to harden our hearts, if we are to survive without being totally overwhelmed by the plight of others. When we cannot distance ourselves from suffering, we are in danger of becoming emotionally exhausted.

Understanding pity

Another word that is sometimes confused with empathy is pity. Pity is a painful feeling aroused in us when we see someone (or an animal) who is being subjected, undeservedly, to something which causes pain or distress. This feeling is how we might feel if we were the object being so treated.

One way of looking at pity, sympathy and empathy, is that pity, the feeling that gives rise to compassion and mercy, is the root feeling. Arising from pity are empathy and sympathy. Thus when pity is aroused we can direct that feeling one of two ways.

- If it is directed inwards we can identify too closely with it, and it becomes sympathy, where we feel *like* the other person. When we do feel like the other person sympathy can paralyse, just as the other person is paralysed. We then may seek to 'do' something for the other person, for in the doing our own feelings are taken care of.

- If we direct it outwards, towards the other person, as empathy, we project our understanding into the situation and the person is energised into doing something for him or herself.

Exploring empathy, sympathy and pity

In the discussion on pity it was suggested that it is the root emotion which gives rise to empathy on the one hand and sympathy on the other. The definition of sympathy suggests that it involves the counsellor too much in your feelings; as if the counsellor has become you.

Both sympathy and empathy mean that we have to be able to enter the inner world of the other person:

- sympathy means that we are more likely to become trapped in the other person's world

- empathy means that we can step back into our own world.

It is this ability which is so crucial in effective counselling.

At the same time, the counsellor cannot be so objective and possessed of such critical insight that he or she fails to respond to your feelings; that is being unsympathetic. Some people find it easier to feel sympathy with someone's sorrow than with another's joy, and for counsellors this may require some exploratory work as to why this should be so.

Part of the counselling process is to bring some objectivity to the relationship, yet too much objectivity creates distance, while too little hampers progress. It means striving for a fine balance between involvement and over-involvement. We feel that one can be objective without being impersonal. At the same time, to become involved demonstrates our humanity. Being involved with another person has its risks. In one training session, counsellor Brian Thorne spoke of how he was in danger of losing his moorings in one interview, as he viewed the enormity of the client's isolation. For Brian, experiencing that isolation was temporarily terrifying. Yet it was probably that momentary identification which enabled him to really enter the client's world and make contact other than with words.

Some people might find it easier to feel in sympathy with the under-dog than with those who are successful, or with those who claim to be victims of colour prejudice and not be able to see both sides of the issue. In all such instances our objectivity might have been influenced by our own life experiences which, in turn, affect judgement. Above all, sympathy and not empathy will cloud judgement and influence decisions and actions in favour of the person for whom we feel sympathy.

- When someone responds to you in pity, you are likely to feel patronised.

- When someone responds to you in sympathy, you are likely to feel misunderstood.

- When someone responds to you in empathy, you are likely to feel empowered.

Communicating empathy
How the counsellor communicates empathy will vary, according to the counsellor and the statement you make, but it must be communicated. If it stays locked up within the counsellor it is of no use to you. An example is when Jane was talking about the death of her marriage, and said she was 'devastated', I responded with, 'I have an image of a lovely building crashing to the ground, and lying in rubble.' That was an accurate reflection of her feelings.

Empathy might be difficult to explain but, like the old Scottish saying, 'It's better felt than telt.'

Exploring empathy in action

The counsellor listens to you on two levels – surface and implied – and identifies and responds to both facts and feelings. When the counsellor responds the response may focus on one level or the other, but the more the counsellor works with implied facts and feelings, the more accurate the empathy is.

But everything doesn't come from the counsellor. However skilled they are the response might not be accurate; that is where you have a vital part to play.

• Do not accept what the counsellor says if it is not precisely what you wanted to say or does not express your feelings exactly.

You won't offend them if you say, 'That is near, but it's not quite right.' Then together you can throw it back and forth until you are satisfied.

Examples of lack of empathy

Marcus feels guilty about being gay
Charles, a clergyman, was listening to Marcus, a recent convert. He was saying how life was proving difficult for him. Marcus disclosed that he was gay. Charles had been brought up to believe that homosexuals were deviants and fully responsible for their sexual preference.

Charles says, 'Homosexuality is a sin, and is the work of the Devil. I must pray with you and cast out the spirit of homo-sexuality.'

Possible obstacles to empathy
• Biases, prejudices, values, beliefs.

• Lack of knowledge of human behaviour.

• Lack of self-awareness.

• An unwillingness to explore.

Jane gets herself into a relationship mess
June, aged 38, is a mature student nurse with one daughter aged 6. June's common-law husband deserted the family six months

before, an event that ended a long history of disharmony and violence. Her college work has gone downhill.

Tim, the college lecturer, says, 'Perhaps what I'm going to say might sound a little harsh, but really June, whatever possessed you in the first place to get involved with that awful man? You knew what he was like, the reputation he had, you've said so and now look at the mess you're in.'

Possible obstacles to empathy
- Loss of respect for the client.

- Biases, prejudices, values, beliefs.

- Not recognising June's relationship needs.

Examples of accurate empathy

1. Kate, a senior nurse teacher, talking to Simon, a colleague
'It's no secret, and you know better than anybody else, I'm a workaholic. I can't remember when I allowed myself to have a day off to do just nothing. It sounds awful when it's put like that. I've been that way for 12 years now. I ought to do something about it, shouldn't I? I'm a free agent. Nobody's making me do it, or holding a gun to my head. I feel caught in a treadmill.'

Simon says, 'Kate, it seems that you've pushed yourself all these

Expressed Facts	**Implied Facts**
Nurse teacher	Lacking enjoyment
Works hard	Self-imposed
Twelve years	Stressed
Her own choosing	Driven
Expressed Feelings	**Implied Feelings**
Regrets	Trapped
Tired	No future
Joyless	Desperation
	Never getting anywhere
	Wasted life

Fig. 4. Example of expressed and implied facts and feelings.

years to get somewhere, and now the driving force has caught up with you. You've put work first in your life and you've forgotten how to relax and enjoy yourself. There seems to be a desperation in your voice as you think about the immediate future, for you can't see any way out of this feeling of being caught like a helpless mouse on some endless conveyer belt of work and more work, and never seeming to get anywhere.'

2. Karen, talking to Betty, a counsellor at the church coffee morning

'I love Jack and my children very much, and I like doing most things around the house. Of course they get boring at times, but on the whole I suppose it can be very rewarding. I don't really miss working, going to the office every day. Most women complain of being just a housewife and just a mother. But then again, I wonder if there's more for me. Others say there has to be. I really don't know.'

Betty says, 'Karen, on the one hand you say you are content with your lot, and on the other I hear a big question mark. For most of the time what you do satisfies you and it's rewarding, yet within that there are moments of boredom. You say you don't miss going to the office, yet I hear a certain wistful longing there for change, something to relieve the boredom and routine. It seems as if there's also a certain feeling of "I'm not sure that I should be saying this, perhaps I'm being disloyal." It seems that you may be feeling that you've reached a stage when you would like to think about something else than just being a mother and a housewife, something to relieve the staleness, yet just thinking about that somehow feels wrong.'

See if you can identify why Betty responded the way she did.

BEING GENUINE

Genuineness, or congruence, is one of the Carl Roger's core conditions. Genuineness means that the counsellor is authentic, real, and true and does not respond from behind a façade of 'the professional counsellor'. There is an honesty and openness about the counsellor's responses which tell you that the person making them is genuine and is not playing out a role.

If the counsellor says, 'I'm feeling a deep sadness at the moment at what you are telling me', you can be certain that this is true, and will be backed up by your own feelings and what you observe of the counsellor.

Although you and the counsellor are in a professional relationship, it is not one of inferior and superior, pupil and teacher; it is one of equals, each making his or her unique contribution to the development of the relationship.

Genuineness means that the counsellor is able to say 'sorry' when perhaps he or she has not heard your deepest feelings, or has taken control and given direction. It also means that you can share a joke and have a laugh; counselling need not be all deadly serious.

Being open

One aspect of genuineness in counselling is that of not denying one's feelings. As with empathy you, the client, will achieve more if you are likewise genuine and do not hide your feelings. Counselling is not detective work, so the counsellor has to rely on what you say, backed up by careful observation and a large element of active intuition. If the counsellor sets out to be open and genuine about how he or she feels, then can you do anything less?

Genuineness on the part of the counsellor does not mean that you will be burdened with the counsellor's problems. Rather, it applies to the relationship between you and the counsellor.

Genuineness might mean the counsellor going out on a limb. For example, Sally was talking in a matter of fact way about not being able to have children. After a few minutes I felt a tug in my stomach and tears pricked my eyes. I said, 'Sally, I feel a deep pain within me right now,' (pointing at my stomach). 'I'm not sure if that's my pain or yours.' Sally began to cry and as she did her pain and anger were released. I made no attempt to offer an interpretation or explanation; just telling how I felt offered Sally the release she needed.

UNDERSTANDING WARMTH

We all know when someone feels warm toward us, and when cold. Yet defining **warmth** is difficult. Generally, warmth is conveyed by words and by our body language. For example, if a person avoids eye contact and does not follow up your response they are conveying non-warmth. The above begs the question – if a person is aloof, can he or she convey warmth? If I maintain an emotional distance, can I demonstrate warmth?

People who are warm are saying, 'I like you.' 'I care for you.' Warmth is not something that can be switched on like an electric light; neither can a person pretend to be warm. People can try, but it will be detected as a sham. At the same time some people do call out our warmth more than others.

When someone who is warm meets a person who is distant, aloof, and cold, the reaction could be withdrawal and a feeling of being pushed away. Thus in counselling, the development of a warm and caring relationship is very much two-way. If you, as client, feel coldness toward your counsellor, it could arise from a desire to keep the counsellor at a distance. The implication of this could be that if you did allow the counsellor to approach closer, then they might discover something about you which you would rather not disclose. Another possibility is that the counsellor is inappropriately warm, and this could frighten you off. Inappropriate warmth is likely to show itself in physical contact.

Looking at physical contact

It is worth digressing a little to examine physical contact. Touch is a powerful way of making emotional contact with people, particularly when they are distressed. Not everybody is comfortable with touch, even when they are distressed. Touch can release feelings; it can also stifle them.

In the course of counselling training, your counsellor will have explored the need for touch, and will be sensitive to how you feel and will not force it on you. Some people do not like shaking hands, so counsellors will even be wary of this common greeting. If you consider the counsellor has overstepped the agreed boundaries, try to find the courage to challenge what has caused you anxiety.

Assessing warmth

To return to warmth. How would you assess your own warmth level? If you are naturally warm you might feel that the counsellor is cold towards you if he or she is not openly warm and seems to keep at a distance. The counsellor who challenges you might seem not to care, and you might feel a lack of warmth, but this could be just what is needed *at that moment*. If the counsellor was over-warm you might not feel able to challenge him or her. So as in all interpersonal work there has to be a balance between over-warmth and being too brisk and business-like.

It is doubtful if your counsellor could convey empathy and be cold, for that would be like a fountain sending out both hot and cold water from the same spout. Thus all the discussion on empathy applies equally to warmth.

Carl Rogers speaks of non-possessive warmth. Possessive warmth is the opposite of what has been discussed above. Possessive warmth is demanding and cloying, and is more for the benefit of the other person than for you. You can detect possessive warmth in that it makes you feel uncomfortable and uneasy; it robs you of energy. It is like an over-hot hot water bottle.

Examples of 'warm' phrases

- Things are beginning to happen.

- There's been some good thinking.

- That's fine.

- That's a new idea to me.

- I knew you could do it.

- I really like that.

- You can do it, I know you can!

- Any more ideas?

- That's a great idea.

- You're on the right track.

- That's a winner.

- I appreciate what you have done.

- Go ahead . . . try it.

- I never thought of that.

- You're on top form.

- You've worked really hard.

UNDERSTANDING ACCEPTANCE

Another aspect of warmth is respect, which is closely linked to **acceptance**. Respect does not mean liking, although it would be difficult to like without also having respect.

Acceptance is more positive than respect. Acceptance, like warmth, is not put on, is not a façade; it is genuine. It is based on the counsellor's firm belief in the uniqueness of every person, in spite of differences, quirks and foibles. The counsellor's acceptance will encompass your strengths and weaknesses, your successes and failures, your different values and expectations, simply because these are what make you the unique individual you are.

The counsellor might not approve of what you do, for approval carries with it a moral judgement, and part of the counsellor's training is to become aware of how moral values can influence interaction with clients. The counsellor who operates from a base of acceptance sees beneath the surface and the behaviours to the real person, and that person is unique. If the counsellor allows his or her values to interfere with the relationship, then they have moved from being impartial to partial, and from acceptance to rejection.

Encouraging acceptance

Acceptance is not like perfect pitch in music – a gift. It is neither a gift nor is it perfect. Most of us would find it easier to accept some people than others. But the counsellor, by virtue of training, experience and often soul-searching, strives to accept clients as they are, to suspend judgement and to put his or her own values on hold so as not to interfere with acceptance.

Acceptance is not a one-way street. It does not all come from the counsellor. If you do not accept yourself you might find it difficult to acknowledge the counsellor's acceptance of you. Accepting yourself does not mean that you are satisfied with yourself as you are and that you should not work for change. One view says we can never change anything until we accept it. We can only truly accept change when we have accepted ourselves as we are.

Learning to work with acceptance

Acceptance is a crucial element in counselling, indeed in any relationship, and being able to recognise when you are not being accepted is one way you can contribute to the relationship. Normally we know when someone is not accepting of us; we feel rejected and put down.

Just as a doctor accepts every piece of information about the patient's physical health as having relevance, so the counsellor accepts everything as relevant about your health and well-being.

To be accepted is one of the strongest needs found in every person; regardless of their circumstance is the need to be accepted – loved for who he or she is. You might care to meditate for a few moments on those people whom you feel accept you, then consider those whom you find it difficult to accept, and why. If you are to get the most out of counselling – working with your counsellor in a partnership – and if you find it difficult to accept your counsellor, you would probably find it constructive to consider the reasons.

Learning to recognise when someone is non-accepting is one way of helping to make sense of relationships. The following exercise will help you focus on acceptance within the counselling relationship.

Identifying your feelings
- How could you tell that someone was not demonstrating acceptance?

- How would you judge if someone was accurately reflecting your feelings?

UNDERSTANDING UNCONDITIONAL POSITIVE REGARD

The fourth core condition of Carl Rogers – **unconditional positive regard** – is rather a mouthful, but essentially it means loving care although Rogers does not use the word love.

- 'Conditional' regard implies that conditions are set on the relationship. Phrases such as 'I will love you if . . .' 'I will not love you if . . .' imply conditional love.

- Unconditional regard means that whatever the person does, says, feels or does not feel, the counsellor will not cease to hold you in high esteem.

That is a tall order for anyone, and rather than always achieving it your counsellor will strive towards this as an ideal. Even if the quality of regard is less than perfect, it still operates.

Regard shows itself in how the counsellor appreciates you. This does not have to be verbalised; in fact, if the counsellor did tell you how much you were appreciated, you might suspect their motives. Regard, of the kind we are talking about, comes through the way the counsellor relates to you, listens to you and is able to convey empathy to you. By this you will feel a person of worth, rather than having to be told it.

Regard is often dependent on whether we like the person or not, and just as often it can vary like the wind. For example, if you feel criticised your regard might swing to the north; if you feel loved, it could swing the other way. That is conditional regard, and it is something the counsellor will strive to avoid and will constantly strive to be consistent.

Experiencing unconditional positive regard
Positive regard helps you to feel safe. Knowing that you are accepted, and that whatever you are or whatever you say will not affect the counsellor's regard for you, is like an anchor in the midst of a storm.

Above all, positive regard is not filtered through the counsellor's feelings and values; it is not conditional upon what is happening in their own life. Neither is it conditional upon your complying with what the counsellor wishes you to be.

SUMMARY

1. One of the most important tasks of your counsellor is to create an atmosphere in which you feel safe enough to say how you feel and to explore whatever it is that has brought you to counselling. This is not so much a skill as a quality of the counsellor, derived from the core conditions of empathy, genuineness, warmth, regard and acceptance.

2. Counsellors work hard to relate with empathy – the ability to get in touch with your feelings, even when they are not expressed. Empathy is a crucial quality in counselling, and is tied into active listening and to being able to hear between the lines. Counsellors are not superhuman and it is likely that they

will get something not quite right. If you, the client, do not say how you feel, the counsellor might never know and you could end up feeling not understood. Look upon counselling as a partnership of equals.

3. An essential part of empathy is the counsellor being able to enter your frame of reference, to see how the world looks through your eyes. The counsellor has to be temporarily willing to step out of his or her own frame of reference. Someone who is not secure in their own world would find it difficult to get anywhere near your frame of reference.

4. Sympathy and pity are similar to but different from empathy. Empathy does not make assumptions of how you feel, but reflects what you say. Sympathy assumes that it knows how you feel because this is how it feels for the sympathiser. Pity is not to be confused with sugary sentimentality. In its true sense it is compassion, and without compassion counselling would be sterile.

5. The other counsellor qualities – genuineness, warmth and regard – are separate yet linked parts of acceptance. Carl Rogers was a humanist, though his early experience is based on Christian teaching. The concept of acceptance is based on a theological conviction that we have an innate dignity and worth which is derived from our relationship to God and that acceptance cannot be lost by any weakness or failure on our part. However, the consciousness and the feeling of one's worth can be lost. In counselling, the client can lose this consciousness and feeling of personal dignity and value if the counsellor loses respect for the client. Acceptance requires the quality of love. The two persons know each other; they know their weaknesses and strengths, their successes and failures, and in spite of them mutual respect continues and even increases. Acceptance is the opposite of rejection, and although the counsellor is not concerned with sin and forgiveness, the principle of acceptance and all that it means is fundamental in the counselling relationship. A person who feels estranged from God and humankind may, through the counselling relationship, experience acceptance and so find a way towards feeling accepted in a wider sense.

4

Making Sense of Your Personality

We all have a personality, yet personality is difficult to define or measure. We attach positive or negative labels to people's personality; we judge it by their body build, the way they walk, talk, dress, the way they wear their hair, the company they keep and so on. We speak of someone as being open or closed, sensitive or hard, of being intellectual or dull, charming or a boor. Yet none of those is enough to adequately describe who you are. For we are all unique individuals, yet there *are* several ways in which you can gain more understanding of who you are.

Knowing something of your personality will help you to get the most out of your counselling, because you will have more understanding of:

- the way you function

- and what influences the way you interact with the counsellor.

A related point is that if you have a good idea of who you are, and what motivates you, you bring more to the counselling partnership. Knowing who you are is **self-awareness**.

EXPLORING SELF-AWARENESS

Engaging in counselling without also developing self-awareness would be like driving a car without understanding the highway code, or what it means to be a safe driver. So far as counselling is concerned, the development of insights and self-awareness are crucial if anything worthwhile is to be achieved.

Self-awareness is becoming aware of your physical, mental, emotional, moral, spiritual and social qualities which, together, make you the person you are. It is seeing how they are working together helps you towards your fullest potential.

Counselling helps you to *explore* who you are. It is doubtful if any of us truly *knows* who we are. Life is a constant discovery of parts of us that have, until that moment, remained hidden from our conscious knowledge. Indeed many of us would rather be thought of by others in a way other than as our true self. This can put us under great pressure. Generally it is less stressful to be true than to be false.

There is no guarantee that being self-aware will bring 'happiness' – a very transient feeling – however it will bring a certain sense of wholeness. You can never say, 'I have arrived,' but 'I am arriving.' Self-knowledge is a quest, and an essential part of counselling.

Self-awareness has been likened to peeling an onion, layer by layer until finally there is nothing. That is a scary picture. Rather, think of self-awareness as in Figure 5.

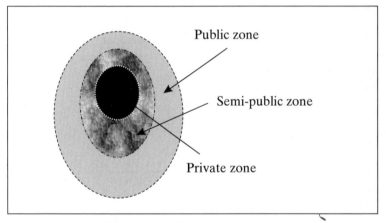

Fig. 5. The self-awareness zones.

The public zone

This is the person people recognise as you. It is the zone into which you are comfortable letting people enter. It is the zone of few secrets; the acquaintance zone, in which you operate when, for example, you travel on public transport.

The semi-public zone

This is the zone of intimacy, of friends, of facts, feelings, experiences which you do not talk about to people on the train. The zone which you share with only a few people. Even there, you keep some things confidential, sharing them only with a selected few.

The private zone
This is the secret zone which you are only dimly aware of, often called the unconscious self. Here lie buried much of what you do not want to remember or recognise, yet it is the zone of tremendous potential for growth. You are usually made aware of the contents through dreams and flashes of insight.

Working in the different zones
In counselling, you and the counsellor start to function in the public zone. You present your problem, and so starts the interaction. The counsellor listens and responds, and you start to build trust, then you relate more of your feelings and the trust deepens as more of the contents within the public zone are explored. Your thoughts and feelings in this zone are more surface than deep, and you are likely to find them easy to discuss.

From time to time, and more so as trust deepens, you will dip into the semi-public zone and reveal deeper feelings. You will feel more free to recount painful experiences and explore their meaning. Here the exploration will take in more profound thoughts and feelings, fantasies, fears, wants and needs, your inner traits (those things that make you tick), your values, beliefs and motives; all those things which influence your behaviour and which are deeply rooted within you.

Counselling does not set out to work with the private zone, and the majority of the work will be done in the two other zones. However, as the discussion in Chapter 1 showed, invariably counselling in the semi-private zone will tap into something from the inner zone. Indeed, all of what we are is influenced by what lies deeper within.

Working at your own pace
The counsellor is not there to probe your deepest secrets, and draw them out like decayed teeth. Unfortunately, the image of the psychoanalyst's darkened consulting room, with the patient lying on a couch, puts many people off the idea of going for counselling. The counsellor does not interrogate you, extracting damaging confessions like some MI5 secret agent. While some counsellors might use a couch, the vast majority do not. Comfortable armchairs are the norm. And it is from within this comfortable atmosphere that you are enabled to explore *what you want to*. If

you decide to stay in the public zone, the counsellor will stay there with you. If you decide to explore the next zone, the counsellor will go with you. At all times the choice is yours.

Becoming more self-aware
As you work more in the semi-private zone, and as what is there is brought into the light, so the outer zone will enlarge and become more accessible to other people. You will find that some of the barriers you needed before to keep you safe are no longer valid. Your ways of interacting with people change and you become more (but appropriately) open. You will become more aware of your behaviour, why you do things or don't do them.

At the same time, self-awareness or self-knowledge does not automatically guarantee you instant success; neither does it mean that you will be free from difficulties for the rest of your life. It is not a wonder drug, but it does work wonders. You have started on the road of self-awareness, you have not arrived. If through counselling you have achieved one tiny bit of insight, you have travelled one section of this road we call self-awareness.

Exercise 1: Exploring how self-aware you are
Taking the three zones in Figure 5:

1. *The public zone.* List what you would be prepared to discuss with your counsellor in the first one or two sessions.
2. *The semi-public zone.* List what you would reserve until you felt you could trust your counsellor. When you have done that, arrange them in priority. Start with number 1 as the least threatening, 10 as being doubtful that you would ever disclose or discuss it.
3. *The private zone.* As the contents of this zone, by nature residing in the unconscious, are not easily accessible, you will not be able to list them in the same way. However, you can still think about this zone, by way of the fears you might have of exploring it. What do you think *might* reside there? The very act of thinking about this might release something from the private zone into the semi-private zone where you can then work on it if you so desire.

EXPLORING ABILITY TO CHANGE

> *God changes not what is in a people, until they change*
> *what is in themselves.*
> (The Koran, Chapter 13, v. 11)

> *If there is anything that we wish to change in the child, we should*
> *first examine it and see whether it is not something that could*
> *better be changed in ourselves.*
> Carl Gustav Jung[3]

These two quotations bring together two opposite yet related views. One is that God alone can change; the other is that generally it is more productive to try to change ourselves than someone else. Indeed, it could be strongly argued that we cannot change other people, as many couples in marriage have discovered to the cost of the relationship. When we try to force change, either on ourselves or on others, the natural inclination is to rebel.

Counselling inevitably involves change. Change can be uncomfortable – for you and for other people, who have come to know you as you are. But if counselling does not produce some change, then of what use is it? The feeling of change is one of the reasons for resistance. Again, this is paradoxical; you want to change, yet the prospect of change creates resistance. Why is this? The example below gives a clue.

Geoffrey is fearful of change
Geoffrey was deeply unhappy with his career, his inability to make friends or to maintain relationships with women. He realised he'd chosen his profession because his parents pushed him into it, and despite obtaining many qualifications he never felt he had achieved enough. He never expressed his true feelings, and only showed others 'a front' designed to please them at all costs.

In spite of this awareness, when he began to consider changing he was terrified of becoming someone completely different. 'Who and what would I be?' he asked.

Becoming more yourself
Change through counselling does not involve becoming someone 'other', it involves becoming more fully yourself. Change involves many, probably all, aspects of who we are. This is a strong

statement, yet it carries tremendous hope and excitement. If change did not involve the whole of us, what effect would it have? If a change in self-awareness did not also mean that we looked at other people differently, would it be of any use? If change in our self-awareness did not foster a change in our behaviour, what use would it be?

Change is seldom easy or simple. Even small changes often bring unexpected consequences, which may involve other people as well as yourself. Growth and self-awareness are changes, and while they will undoubtedly benefit you, other people might have difficulty accommodating what is taking place in your life. People on the periphery of your life are not so affected as those close to you. If you are in a relationship, for example, your self-development may create changes, producing tensions because the old familiar ground is no longer common to you and the other person.

Thus change requires much acceptance and accommodation from others, yet at the same time, it requires patience and self-understanding on your part too. Things that were once essential to you may assume less importance and vice versa. If you find that change brings you into conflict with parts of yourself, then this is an indication that you have work yet to do to resolve the conflict. If you find yourself in conflict with someone else, likewise there is work still to do. Part of your overall change might be to work towards resolution with someone else, and in that you might find that you have helped someone else along the road to change.

Embracing change
Change involves shifts in thinking, feelings, behaviour, values, beliefs and attitudes. These are the pillars of your personality and it is these which have formed you the way you are, thus any change in one will have a knock-on effect on the others. If, as a result of counselling, you learn to express your feelings more than you did in the past, and if those feelings make real contact with other people, then this results in a change in the way you think and behave; for it to be otherwise would be a nonsense.

If your thinking has been negative and you constantly put yourself down, if you always looked on the black side of life and counselling helps you to be more positive, then this will affect your feelings and so on. Every part of you – personality, character, temperament – is delicately connected, so that change in one area affects all others.

An illustration can be drawn from the human body. Each part of the body is influenced by every other part. If you prick your finger with a thorn, it is not just the finger that suffers; every part of you is aware of it. If that prick turns poisonous, then the poison will travel throughout the body. When medication is given, it does not just affect the poisoned finger, every part of the body is touched and healed.

Change is inevitable in life. Some changes are welcome, others, like old age, might not be so welcomed depending on one's point of view. Change in counselling is inevitable and it is likely to affect your relationships in some way.

Exercise 2: Deciding what you want to change

Before you engage in counselling it would help you and your counsellor if you could think of specific things in your life where you want change to take place, or the areas where you do not want change.

What I want to change about my thinking:

_____

What I want to change about my feelings:

_____

What I want to change about my behaviour:

_____

What I want to change about my values:

_____

What I want to change about my beliefs:

_____

What I want to change about my attitudes:

_____

What I want to change about the way I relate to people:

CASE STUDIES

Dave changes his attitude to work

Dave was in his mid-20s, in a well-paid engineering job. He came for counselling because he felt under stress. In the course of exploring his life-style it became clear that he was driven by a deep-seated need to achieve. Together we traced this to the demands placed upon him by his adopted parents. His self-awareness developed along the lines that he needed the approval of his parents, but that this approval was acting like a tyrant. The change in his behaviour was that by learning deep relaxation, and practising it regularly, and using a well-developed imagination, he was able to reduce his stress levels to live his life more comfortably.

Meg undergoes change

Meg came for counselling. 'Not that I have any specific problem,' she said at our first contact. However, it quickly became apparent that Meg was in a difficult marriage, with a husband who physically abused her. Yet Meg felt trapped by the constraints of her family and her in-laws, and the church, plus having two children. 'Maybe he will change,' she said. Meg eventually found the strength to end the marriage. This might seem a negative outcome, but the point is that the change Meg underwent meant that she found the courage to take action.

EXPLORING PERSONALITY PREFERENCES

Over many years people have presented different ways of looking at personality, some of which are comprehensive but complicated. One whose popularity hinges on its simplicity and immediate 'Aha! that's me' factor is Personality Types, developed by Isabel Briggs-Myers. In *Gifts Differing* Briggs-Myers extends Jung's work, giving four dimensions with eight preferences: extraversion and introversion; sensing and intuition; thinking and feeling; judgement and perception. For readers who would like to add to their understanding of personality typing, *Please Understand Me* by David Keirsey and Marilyn Bates provides a detailed self-scoring questionnaire.

- Extraversion/introversion is the way we relate to the world around us.

- Sensing/intuition is the way we perceive the world.

- Thinking/feeling is the way we make judgements.

- Judgement/perception is the way we make decisions.

An overview of the eight preferences

Everybody possesses all eight preferences, though the degree to which they are present varies from person to person. As you read through the eight types, try to assess if you are more one than its opposite. And try to work out in what circumstances you rely more on the other preference. Please do not think that any one preference is better or worse than its opposite. We all need each of them if we are to live a balanced life.

Extraversion (E)
People who are more extraverted than introverted:

- are generally sociable and outgoing

- relate to people and things around them

- endeavour to make their decisions in agreement with other people

- are interested in variety and in working with people

- may become impatient with long, slow tasks

- do not mind being interrupted by people

- are usually relaxed and confident

- are usually people of action

- tend to be practical achievers

- feel more at home doing than with ideas.

Introversion (I)
People who are more introverted than extraverted:

- prefer making decisions independently of other people

- tend to be quiet, diligent at working alone

- tend to be socially reserved

- dislike being interrupted while working

- are liable to forget names and faces

- tend to be reserved and questioning

- are interested in what is happening within themselves

- are good at the abstract and ideas

- tend to bottle up feelings

- tend not to be very practical.

Sensing (S)
People who are more sensing than intuitive:

- prefer what is concrete, real, factual, structured, tangible, here-and-now

- tend to mistrust their intuition

- think in careful, detail-by-detail accuracy, very observant

- remember real facts and make few errors of fact

- may miss a grasp of the overall

- tend to be lovers of pleasure; love life

- live in and for the present

- can be accused of being frivolous

- are very conscientious

- are not comfortable using imagination.

Intuition (N) (Written as N because I has been used with Introversion)
People who have more intuition than sensing:

- prefer possibilities, theories, patterns, the overall, inventions and the new

- become bored with the nitty-gritty details, the concrete and actual

- facts must relate to concepts

- think and discuss in spontaneous leaps of intuition

- not very observant of detail

- problem-solving comes easily

- may show a tendency to make errors of fact

- crave inspiration and the novel

- are very imaginative

- tend to be restless and always seeking out something new.

Thinking (T)
People with more thinking than feeling (head types):

- make judgements about life, people, occurrences, and things based on logic, analysis and hard evidence

- avoid irrationality, sentiment, and decisions based on feelings and values

- are interested in logic, analysis and verifiable conclusions

- are less comfortable with empathy, values and personal warmth

- may step on others' feeling and needs without realising it

- often neglect to take into consideration the values of others

- are often considered impersonal

- more likely to believe that their decisions are right and others' wrong

- tend to be businesslike rather than friendly

- are often more truthful than tactful.

Feeling (F)
People with more feeling that thinking (heart types):

- make judgements about life, people, occurrences and things based on empathy, warmth and personal values
- are more interested in people and feelings than in impersonal logic, analysis and things
- conciliation and harmony are more important than being on top or achieving impersonal goals
- get along with people in general
- usually strong in social skills
- often find it difficult to be businesslike
- are generally good talkers, but may ramble
- often find it difficult to work to a structure
- tend to consider feeling is superior to thinking
- often more tactful than truthful.

Judgement (J)
People with more judgement than perception:

- decisive, firm, and sure
- like setting goals and sticking to them
- want to make decisions and get on to the next project
- will leave an unfinished project behind and go on to new tasks and not look back, if that's what has to be done
- give priority to work over play
- are good at meeting deadlines
- tend to be judgemental of themselves and other people
- tend not to like the unexpected
- like to get things settled and out of the way
- tend to think they know what other people should do.

Perception (P)
People who have more perception than judgement:

- always want to know more before making decisions and judgements

- open, flexible, adaptive, non-judgemental

- able to appreciate all sides of an issue

- always welcome new perspectives and new information about issues

- difficult to pin down

- hate working to deadlines

- often so indecisive and noncommittal that they frustrate themselves and other people

- often involved in many tasks

- give priority to play rather than work

- often need to be forced into making a decision.

Exercise 3: Making an assessment of your type

Your type is made up of whichever of the four preferences are dominant. Having worked through the eight preferences, are you able to decide if you are:

- More E than I or vice versa?

- More S than N or vice versa?

- More T than F or vice versa?

- More J than P or vice versa?

My type . . . .

How your personality preferences might influence counselling

- People who are too extraverted often get on people's nerves; someone who is too introverted often has difficulty making contact with people at all.

- People who are high on sensing can get so caught up in counting the trees that they miss the beauty of the wood; people who are too intuitive often seem 'away with the fairies'.

- People who are too high on thinking often intellectualise everything; people who are too high on feeling often swamp others by their warmth.

- People who are too high on judgement often become judge, jury and executioner; people who are too high on perception often give the impression of being grown up children.

These are generalisations. However, how you interact with your counsellor, and your understanding of what is going on, could be significantly enhanced by knowing why you prefer certain ways of working above others. All of this increases your self-awareness, helping you to make more sense of counselling.

Effective counselling might require you to work towards making changes in the way you relate to the world, how you perceive the world, the way you make judgements and the way you make decisions. Even small changes can work wonders.

What follows demonstrates how each of the eight preferences may help or hinder counselling.

Extraverts (E)/introverts (I)

The E part of you will tend to accept change with enthusiasm, mainly because change brings with it the possibility of new relationships. If anything, the extravert may rush into change with open arms before counting the cost. The E part of us likes to talk, to hold the floor, but might have trouble listening.

The I part of you proceeds with caution. Change for the introvert brings more questions than answers, and that is un-settling. The I part likes to take things in, digest them, and only then speak and the response is given with caution. The E part would be less comfortable with silence than the I part, which might prompt you to say anything just to keep things moving. The E part tends not to like reflection, which is one of the strengths of the I.

Sensing (S)/intuition (N)

The S part of you tends to resist change, because it disturbs the status quo. When the S part cannot find the next logical piece in the plan, there is anxiety. S needs to know what is, to have hands on. The S is cautious and rarely jumps to conclusions, and often needs careful explanations and to work through logical stages.

The N part of you enjoys possibilities, revels in the unknown and new beginnings. N is creative, change energises. Because the N sees things with the intuition, it often jumps ahead to make what might seem illogical conclusions, but which are often correct. The S prefers to work with the obvious; the N is comfortable working with the imagination.

Thinking (R)/feeling (F)

T asks is it true or false. Analysis requires time, so if change is hurried, before the logic is fully accepted, it will produce stress and will be rejected. Thus if something is not logical it is likely that you will feel irritated. You would prefer to debate than to discuss your feelings. You will generally want to make judgements based on logic and reason.

F asks is it agreeable or disagreeable. Change would be acceptable provided there was sufficient attention paid to the 'human' aspect, and that there was ample time for discussion. The F tends to become irritated if asked to be too logical and reasoning. Feelings are what makes the world go round, not cold logic.

Judgement (J)/perception (P)

The J part excels in plans, decisions and conclusions. If change is protracted by people who can't make up their minds, stress is likely to occur. The J part will plan an event well in advance and expect other people to comply. The J part puts work first and is often judgemental of people.

The P part puts off making decisions. Open-mindedness is a P strength. Putting perceptive people under pressure, such as deadlines, will create stress. The J part would be comfortable working towards set goals, whereas the P part would find it difficult to look that far ahead, as they prefer to live in the moment.

Although we have presented the eight preferences as if they were separate entities, each is modified by all the other preferences. However, having an idea of your basic preferences is one way of making sense of what is happening.

EXPLORING TYPE A AND B PERSONALITIES

Competitiveness is a characteristic of what has become known as **Type A** personality. **Type B** people are less competitive. It seems that type A people are constantly striving for something, although it is not always clear what, and whatever it is drives them with a high degree of urgency. One of the findings is that such people are more prone to build up of stress.

Are you type A or type B?

From the list given, score an A for every time you answer 'mostly', and B for every time you would answer 'rarely', to the statements on page 78.

Very few people are totally A or B; most of us are a mixture. It depends in what circumstances we are one or the other. It is not 'wrong' to be very type A, and there is no particular merit in being totally type B. As in all aspects of life, what is important is achieving balance. Many people tend to concentrate on the nega-tive aspects of being one type or the other, yet there are also positives.

Identifying some advantages of being type A

- You get things done.

- You have lots of drive.

- You have a tendency to succeed in your chosen career.

- You are self-directed.

- You can express your opinions.

- You are likely to be a good leader.

- You are likely to be good in an emergency or crisis.

- You can juggle conflicting tasks.

- You can stand up for yourself and others.

Identifying some advantages of being type B

- You are a good team member and don't mind taking orders.

- You tend towards being patient in most situations.

- You are not overly ambitious, thus more satisfied with life.

- You are good at paying attention to detail.

Statement	A	B
I have a high need to achieve and to excel		
I am highly competitive in almost everything		
I often experience muscle tension around the neck and back		
I am far from satisfied with life		
I am highly organised and don't take life as it comes		
I am excessively responsible, serious, and conscientious		
I believe that 'time is money' and shouldn't be wasted		
I like juggling several demanding tasks at once		
I get a 'buzz' out of having to think things through rapidly		
I have no hesitation in forcefully expressing opinions		
I could be described as being totally dedicated to my job		
I often race against the clock to get things done		
I am motivated by ambition		
I get impatient waiting around for people		
I often complete people's sentences for them		
My behaviour is challenging and forceful		
Other people's opinions and recognition are important to me		
Success is all-important		
I walk, eat, talk and live at a rapid pace		
Work takes priority over all other interests		
Total both columns		
Final score A =	B =	

- You like co-operating with people.

- You can usually see both sides of an argument.

How being type A might hinder counselling
- Interrupting the counsellor and not really listening.

- Thinking too far ahead and not really considering what has been said.

- Trying to get it right and be a quick, clever client, without realising there is not a 'right/good' way to be.

- Finding it more difficult to express your pain, hurt or sadness than your anger and resentment.

- Wanting quick solutions, rather than taking time to stay with the discomfort which would bring deeper awareness.

- Being so controlled that you resist what is happening in counselling.

How being type B might hinder counselling
- Being inclined to let the counsellor take the lead and do the work all of the time.

- Investing your counsellor with superior powers, thus not affirming your own power.

- Being co-operative to the point where you agree with all your counsellor's tentative suggestions, regardless of whether they feel accurate to you.

- Finding it difficult to take action towards change.

- Being unable to acknowledge your own power and potential.

- Finding it more difficult to express your anger and resentment than pain, hurt or sadness.

CO-OPERATING IN THE COUNSELLING PROCESS

Co-operation, not competition, is essential in counselling. If you are a competitive person, you might find yourself competing with the counsellor. The counsellor will not imply that he or she knows better than you, yet in the exploration of your feelings, life experiences or in exploring alternatives, you might feel a need to compete, especially if you feel the counsellor has not understood precisely what you mean. If this happens, try to remember that the counsellor is not a competitor or rival trying to score points. Counselling assumes co-operation, not competition, not only from the counsellor but from you, and is based on mutual respect. Courage, consideration, caring and sharing provide a foundation from which co-operation can be developed.

In the course of their training counsellors will have challenged themselves and been challenged about competitive attitudes. If a counsellor were to be highly competitive he or she might in turn engage you in a win/lose relationship. However, if you do find yourself feeling competitive during counselling, and the counsellor does not 'play the game', the conflict thus generated could very well be the spark to kindle the desire to change.

Avoiding competing with your counsellor

- Clarify your goals, and make sure they are relevant.

- Develop the skills of active, empathic listening.

- Stop working on counter-arguments while your counsellor is speaking.

- Take the risk of being open to what the counsellor is saying.

- Try tuning in to the counsellor's point of view.

- Explore with the counsellor the roots of your competitiveness.

CASE STUDY

Kieran becomes less competitive

Kieran was the youngest of a large family. In his work at the university he, in his own words, 'kept his nose to the grindstone.' He achieved good grades, but in this third year he found the stress getting to him. As we talked he said that his father, a bank manager, was never satisfied with Kieran's grades. When he took ten O levels, and got six grade As and four Bs, his father said, 'And what happened to the other four?' Father was himself driven by a strong work ethic, and this had rubbed off on Kieran. Over several months Kieran was able to let up on his desire to 'show Dad that I can be as good as him.' He learnt how to relax, to engage in limited social activity. Above all, Kieran found that he could laugh.

SUMMARY

1. Personality is the characteristic patterns of behaviour, thought and emotion that determine your adjustment to your environment. These characteristics are significantly stable over a period of time. Counselling does not aim to change your personality, but if you can change one little bit of the way you think, feel and behave you will have achieved a great deal.

2. If your aim in counselling is to increase your self-awareness, and if you gain one insight, you will have achieved a great deal. Self-awareness is not something you acquire, like buying a new house; it might mean letting go of old thought patterns or ways of relating to people, and adopting new ones. This takes place over a long period of time, and the process will continue until you die. Self-awareness is not automatic, and does not necessarily equate with age. You decide to set out on the pathway of self-awareness, and all the time you tread it, you move further along that road.

3. Counselling involves change, otherwise what use is it? The questions you must ask (and the word 'must' is anathema in counselling, so it is used here deliberately) before and during counselling are: 'What about me do I want or need to change? What must I change? What am I unhappy about with myself that I could change? What do I definitely do not want to change? What will happen if I change? What will happen if I don't change? What can I afford to change? What can I not afford to change?' Asking these questions will ensure that you are in the driving seat during counselling.

4. One of many models of personality types defines eight preferences. Try to relate what you have learnt here to your own life. You might be tempted to start analysing other people; try to avoid playing the amateur psychologist and concentrate on yourself. Note in which circumstances, and with whom, you behave in a certain way; by doing this you will be developing your self-awareness. Not all development takes place during

your counselling sessions. Take charge of your own life, and use the counselling sessions to build on what has been happening in between.

5. Neither competition nor co-operation is inherently good or bad; it is the use we put them to. If you are 'terribly co-operative' to the extent that you never have an opinion of your own, or you become a doormat for other people to walk all over, that is not healthy. Co-operation is a partnership; being a human doormat is bondage. Competition in sport is essential, yet even there if it shuts out all other aspects of life it has become tyrannical. Competition in personal relationships, of which counselling is one, is subversive. If your personal relationships are characterised by competition, that could be one of the areas for exploration. Understanding the roots of that competition might be enough for you to make adjustments and improve your relationships.

5

Deciding Which Approach Suits You Best

Deciding which counsellor to approach might not be easy. Looking in *Yellow Pages* is one way, personal recommendation is another, but even then understanding what to expect will make the choice easier. This chapter will take you through the principal counselling approaches. Knowing how counsellors work will help you to make a more informed choice. We shall explore five approaches to counselling, then discuss goals and goal-setting.

One way of defining the differences between approaches is to consider where their primary focus is, on:

- feelings

- thinking

- behaviour

- or a combination of these.

Put simply:

- Psychodynamic and person-centred approaches concentrate on feelings.

- Behaviourists believe that if the behaviour (including thinking) is adjusted, all other aspects will be put to rights.

- Cognitive theories (mainly concerned with thinking) put forward the view that all behaviour is primarily determined by what a person thinks.

- An eclectic or integrated counsellor may use all or any of these theories and approaches.

In this highly over-simplified introduction to the three main focuses, it may seem that a counsellor who uses one approach only may ignore vital parts of the client – like thinking or behaviour, if the focus is on feelings – but that is not so. What distinguishes one type of counselling from another is where the attention is focused, and the techniques and skills used.

UNDERSTANDING THE PSYCHODYNAMIC APPROACH

Freud's psychoanalysis gave rise to the word **psychodynamic**, which means every psychological theory which uses the concept of inner drives and the interaction of mental forces within the psyche. Thoughts, feelings and behaviours are viewed as manifestations of inner drives.

Psychodynamic counselling derives from psychoanalysis, but is not psychoanalysis.

A psychodynamic approach is the systematised knowledge and theory of human behaviour and its motivation. Inherent in this is the study of the functions of emotions. Psychodynamic counselling recognises the role of the unconscious, and how it influences behaviour. Further, behaviour is determined by past experience, genetic endowment and what is happening in the present.

In psychodynamic counselling the counsellor is far less active than in many other approaches, and relies more on you bringing forth material, rather than reflecting feelings and inviting exploration, and what you disclose will be interpreted according to psychoanalytic model. Just as in psychoanalysis the patient is expected to report anything that comes to mind, so in psychodynamic counselling. Hesitation to reveal is interpreted as resistance, which must be worked through before progress is achieved.

Exploring insight

While feelings are not ignored – for to ignore them would be to deny an essential part of the person – feelings are not the emphasis – **insight** is, and that insight relates to the functioning of the unconscious. For the underlying belief is that it is the un- conscious that produces dysfunction. Thus insight, in the psychodynamic model, is:

- getting in touch with the unconscious

- and bringing what is unconscious into the conscious.

Although insight is usually worked towards in those approaches which focus on feelings, in the psychodynamic approach it is considered essential. You achieve insight when you understand what is causing a conflict. The premise is that if insight is gained, conflicts will cease. Insight is often accompanied by catharsis, which is the release of emotion, often quite dramatic.

Insight refers to the extent to which you become aware of your problems, origins, and influences. It may be sudden – like the flash of inspiration, the 'eureka experience'. More usually it develops stage-by-stage as you develop psychological strength to deal with what is revealed. The counsellor cannot give you insight. You must arrive at it by yourself.

Nothing is more thrilling than when an insight dawns. It may have lingered for days or weeks, gradually working away in the subconscious, even figuring in your dreams, or with little flashes of sub-insights – something like looking through frosted glass. There the vision is dimmed; the form can be distinguished, but lacks detail. Thus with some insights. Not all come like bolts from the blue.

Working with a psychodynamic counsellor

Psychodynamic counsellors are trained to interpret what you say through the psychoanalytic model, and while the counsellor will not analyse you, neither will he or she become as involved as in some other approaches. The psychodynamic counsellor can appear distant and detached, possibly even lacking in warmth, but this is because of the belief that the personal qualities of the counsellor should not intrude into the counselling relationship.

UNDERSTANDING BEHAVIOURAL COUNSELLING

Behavioural counsellors are those who work with you to change the way you behave by concentrating on the behaviour itself, rather than dealing with the thoughts or feelings that might be connected to the behaviour. For example, to treat fear of heights a strict behaviour therapist may gradually expose you to greater and greater heights, letting you adjust yourself each time to the new height until you no longer react to heights with fear. This sort of approach is also called behaviour modification.

Emotional or behavioural problems are considered the consequences of faulty learned behaviour patterns. The aim of behaviour modification, therefore, is to change behaviour patterns by having you learn new behaviours, or relearn or unlearn old behaviours. Although this is the classical view, most behaviour therapists now acknowledge the role of thoughts and feelings in shaping behaviour, but the thrust will still be towards behavioural change, rather than focusing on feelings.

Having set the scene, a brief introduction to what might be involved now follows. It can only be short and generalised, for the counsellor will design a programme suitable for your specific needs. Much of behaviour therapy is short-term – 25 to 50 sessions.

Although each counsellor has his or her individual style, a fairly typical approach would include a detailed analysis of your problems with particular reference to how your behaviour is affected. You and the counsellor will set specific treatment goals. The treatment plan will use appropriate behavioural techniques. The treatment plan will be implemented only after full discussion with you. This is because unless you are fully committed to the change, it will not be successful. When the treatment plan has run its course, you and the counsellor will evaluate what has been achieved.

Summarising the main features of behavioural counselling

- Concentrates on behaviour rather than on the underlying causes of the behaviour.

- Believes behaviour is learned, and may be unlearned.

- Believes behaviour is susceptible to change through psychological principles, especially learning methods.

- The setting of clearly defined treatment goals.

- Classical personality theories are rejected.

- The counsellor adapts methods to suit the client's needs.

- The focus is on the 'here and now'.

Understanding what desensitisation means

Quite simply, desensitisation aims to reduce or remove sensitivity to something specific that causes a problem, for example allergies. The same behavioural principle is applied in the treatment of anxiety and phobic behaviours.

If this is appropriate for you, under relaxed conditions the counsellor will set up a series of situations that increasingly approximate to the anxiety-provoking one, until anxiety is no longer produced.

Part of the general treatment for anxiety is to teach you how to relax. Relaxation does not mean reading a book, or watching a video or going for a walk. What the counsellor means by relaxation is you being able to relax your whole body, and your mind; the recommendation is that you practise this as near as possible at set times of the day.

In the initial stages, the counsellor and you will have identified the situations which generate anxiety for you, and together you will arrange these in a hierarchy, ranked according to the level of anxiety they evoke, from least to greatest. For example you might find that walking the dog along the river produces mild anxiety, and even thinking about flying in a plane sends your heart racing. In between you might have been able to identify several other situations which create anxiety and with which you find it difficult to cope.

Having identified the anxiety-provoking situations, and worked out your hierarchy, when you are relaxed the counsellor will present to you the least anxiety-provoking situation. When you feel anxious the counsellor will stop, and help you to relax, before continuing. As you confront the least fear and master that, you are strengthened and encouraged to tackle the next situation. Gradually, possibly over weeks or even months, you will work up the hierarchy to the situation which produces the greatest fear.

Case study: Bert copes by using deep relaxation

On the day William was writing this chapter, Bert telephoned him. Several years ago William produced a tape in which he takes the listener through deep relaxation. Bert's daughter, who had been a student of William's, bought one of the tapes to give to her dad. Bert said, 'I've used it every night for the past two years. Now it's broken. I need another.' William has no idea of Bert's particular difficulty, but 20 minutes easy listening helps him sleep.

Identifying problems suitable for behavioural counselling

Behavioural counselling does not ignore the importance of the counselling relationship. Indeed, if you feel supported within a trusting relationship you will generally work conscientiously through the programme. Behaviour therapy is applicable over a full range of problems, for example:

- anxiety disorders
- cardiovascular disease (heart and blood vessels)
- childhood disorders
- depression
- hypertension (high blood pressure)
- interpersonal/marital
- obesity
- sexual disorders
- speech difficulties
- stress management
- substance abuse
- tension headaches.

UNDERSTANDING COGNITIVE COUNSELLING

Cognitive counselling concentrates on what and how you think. There is an old adage – what you think, you become. This is the basic premise upon which is built the cognitive approach:

- what you think influences your feelings and behaviour.

A simple demonstration will illustrate the truth of this. If you recall an unpleasant experience, and concentrate on it, think of all the details, the place, the people, the time, your age when it happened and so on, you will find that you begin to experience the same feelings as you did then. If you take notice of your body, you are likely to find the tell-tale signs of maybe fear, despair or sadness.

Cognitive counselling is particularly useful in combating the negative thought patterns which frequently accompany depression, where thoughts of low self-worth and self-esteem are a common feature. Cognitive therapy works on the premise that thoughts of low self-worth are incorrect and are due to faulty learning. Such thoughts often centre around such negative thoughts as:

- 'I haven't achieved anything'
- 'I have nothing to offer'
- 'I deserve to be criticised'.

The aim of counselling is to help you get rid of faulty concepts that influence negative thinking, so that you start to create positive thoughts, and positive feelings and behaviours. People who live their lives on a negative plane evaluate almost everything negatively; this not only gets them down but pulls other people down as well.

The counsellor will encourage you to learn decision-making and problem-solving skills as part of the process of thinking rehabilitation. If you compare yourself unfavourably with other people, engage in anticipating that the worst is going to happen, then cognitive counselling could help you turn your thinking, feelings and behaviour around. The challenge you have to face is: to change or not to change? The counsellor works to help you replace 'tunnel thinking' with 'lateral, flexible thinking'.

Identifying the challenge of cognitive counselling

One of the skills which all counsellors use is challenging, not to a fight but to encourage you to look at what you are doing or saying, particularly picking up contradictions. Something like, 'You said earlier that you were looking forward to the divorce, now you're saying you'll be devastated. Your feelings are in conflict; maybe we could look at the contradiction.' Challenging has to be done within an emphathic relationship, otherwise it will be perceived as a threat. This applies equally in cognitive counselling, where empathy is essential.

The counsellor will help you challenge the discrepancies between your thoughts, feelings and behaviours within and outside of counselling. False logic and irrational beliefs contribute to faulty thinking.

One particular challenge is that of replacing irrational thinking with rational. Here are two examples.

Irrational   It is easier to avoid difficulties than to
                         face life and responsibilities.

Reconstructed	I know that if I avoid responsibilities I'm only putting off what I must do. I must not make excuses to myself, or blame others for what I don't do.
Irrational	I need something, or someone, stronger or greater than myself to rely on.
Reconstructed	I know I need other people, but if I rely too much on them, my own judgements and my specific needs might not be met.

Identifying what you can do to help yourself

Explore and list your negative thoughts
- When do you think them?

- Is there a pattern?

- Do they occur all the time or only at specific times?

- Are they concerned with specific people or events?

- Do you always lose out and come off worse?

Use imagination
Imagination is a powerful ally. Whenever a negative thought occurs imagine the situation, then change the scene into something positive.

Use 'thought stop'
Every time a negative thought intrudes, say (aloud, if you are able) 'STOP!' If thoughts are particularly troublesome, wear a loose elastic band on your wrist, and when the thought comes snap the elastic. Gradually you will learn to take control of your thoughts.

Substitute
Replace the invasive negative thought with a positive one. Substitution, coupled with imagination, is a powerful way to change from negative to positive thinking. Positive thinking can become as much a habit as negative thinking has been.

UNDERSTANDING PERSON-CENTRED COUNSELLING

The fourth main approach is person-centred counselling, based on the person-centred philosophy of the American psychologist Carl Rogers (1902–1987). Dissatisfied with psychoanalysis, Rogers, believing that diagnosis, planning and interpretation are more for the analyst than for the clients (called patients), started to think what it meant to be a client and to see things from the client's perspective, rather than try to get the client to conform to some theory. Rogers began to:

- listen

- understand

- and reflect what he thought the client was feeling.

-

  This was something revolutionary in therapy, or as he called it, counselling. What Rogers discovered (and here we are talking about 50 years ago, before the proliferation of counselling, a term which most people now accept and have some knowledge of) that his clients (he rapidly moved away from calling them patients) responded with deep feelings of personal involvement and disclosure of what was important *to them*.

> The person-centred approach, then, is primarily a way of being which finds its expression in attitudes and behaviours that create a growth-promoting climate. It is a basic philosophy rather than simply a technique or a method. When this philosophy is lived it helps the person to expand the development of his or her own capacities. When it is lived it also stimulates constructive change in others. It empowers the individual, and when this personal power is sensed, experiences show that it tends to be used for personal and social transformation.
>
> Carl Rogers[4]

Identifying the aim of person-centred counselling

The aim of person-centred counselling is to engage you in an equal partnership, a philosophy that fits very well into the idea of a partnership between you and your counsellor. The counsellor provides a supportive, non-judgemental understanding atmosphere, but will not advise, interpret or direct you.

The person-centred approach emphasises your capacity and strengths to direct the course and direction of your own counselling. You have the ability to solve your problems, however massive they seem. The more the counsellor understands what something means *to you*, the deeper the relationship in which you experience the core conditions (as in Chapter 3), the more in charge you feel. And the more empowered you feel the more able you are to tackle whatever difficulties you are experiencing. The focus is on:

- engaging your frame of reference

- and understanding and tracking precisely what something means to you.

This does not mean that the counsellor is passive. Being able to enter your frame of reference means active listening and a continual struggle to lay aside preconceptions that would hinder the process. The counsellor will help you find the answers to two basic questions:

- 'Who am I?'

- and 'How can I become myself?'

The person-centred counsellor places you firmly at the centre; it is you who are important and at all times the counsellor will strive to understand what something means to you. This arises from the fundamental belief that you have the capacity to understand what it is that is causing you unhappiness or distress. You are the best expert on yourself.

The counsellor's part is to be totally present as a person, not as a counsellor who is all-knowing, but one who is authentic and in a real relationship with you, in which you feel a person of worth.

The person-centred counsellor will not interpret your unconscious motives or conflicts, as a psychodynamic counsellor would do, or attempt to modify your behaviour as a behavioural counsellor would do, but simply reflect what you feel about your thoughts and feelings. The more you do this, the more other feelings will come into awareness which can then be acknowledged.

Identifying your part in the counselling

Within the person-centred relationship you are free to leave, come back, or not return, without judgement or criticism. The counsellor will seek clarification of whatever you say, not for their benefit but for yours. This is done without judgement and not necessarily so that you will elaborate on your feelings. The very fact of hearing your feelings as perceived by the counsellor is often enough to make them clear to you.

It is very likely that in the early stage of person-centred counselling you will spend time describing your problem, but during the course of counselling you will increasingly show understanding of your problem. Also, as you progress through counselling you will feel more comfortable expressing feelings, and your understanding of your feelings will deepen.

When you feel that your thoughts, feelings and behaviours are being received without judgement, at that moment you will know that they are being listened to and understood. When you feel accepted, and when the core conditions are present, you feel safe enough to explore your problems and gradually come to experience those parts of yourself you normally keep hidden – from yourself and others.

Although person-centred counsellors do not use techniques, or problem-solving skills, this does not mean that the counsellor is not skilful. Indeed, it is quite the reverse; staying with you every step of the way requires a great deal of skill, as well as a deep sense of personal awareness.

Summarising the person-centred philosophy

- Every individual has the internal resources for growth.

- When a counsellor demonstrates the core conditions of empathy, non-possessive warmth, unconditional positive regard and genuineness, therapeutic movement will take place naturally.

- Human nature is essentially social and essentially constructive.

- Self-regard is a basic human need.

- Persons are motivated to seek truth.

- Perceptions determine experience and behaviour.

- The client should be the focus in the helping relationship.

- People should be related to as whole persons who are in the process of becoming. People should be respected as doing their best to grow and to preserve themselves, given their current internal and external circumstances.

- It is important to reject the pursuit of authority or control over others and to seek, instead, to share power.

Taken from D. Mearns and B. Thorne[5]

CASE STUDY

Vicky experiences person-centred counselling

Now follows some extracts of interviews with Vicky. She had been referred by her GP for anxiety following an exploratory operation for a lump in her abdomen, which proved to be non-cancerous. Vicky, who has never married, is approaching retirement as a headteacher and finds the prospect terrifying. In the second session she has been talking about lack of control.

Counsellor So then if we look at that a bit closer, you feel that something is, or has been controlling you.

Vicky Mmm. I suppose you could say that. Thinking about that, it's this worry, isn't it? Silly really, letting something like that take control.

Counsellor Like a tyrant. Almost like keeping you in prison.

Vicky That is very accurate. In fact over the past year I have felt like a prisoner. If I didn't have my job to go to, and all the other things, I wouldn't want to go out. I mean, I'm all right when I am out, as if I've escaped, but it's when the door closes, then I feel trapped.

Counsellor As if the cell door clangs behind you?

Vicky (*Her lip trembling*) Yes, as if I've committed some terrible crime. And I feel so alone.

Counsellor Isolated and cut off from all human contact.

Vicky (*Reaching for a tissue*) Silly isn't it? Why should I feel like this? I mean, so isolated, yet I keep very busy.

Later in the session Vicky, speaking of her work, says:

Vicky (*Crying*) I don't want it to end. My whole life has been teaching. I've had hundreds of children, even though they weren't mine. If only . . .

Counsellor If only?

Vicky Yes, if only. Could this be connected? It's not something I talk about, and it happened a long time ago.

Counsellor You seem to have made a connection between how you feel now and something in your past life, yet you are hesitant about expressing it.

Vicky discloses that several years before she had had an affair with a married man, who had died in a climbing accident. This had been gnawing away at her over the years, the more so as she was friendly with the widow, and god-mother to the daughter. Much of what then takes place relates to Vicky's need to forgive herself, as well as talking through her anxiety about retirement.

At no time in these brief extracts does the counsellor go beyond what Vicky is talking about. No probing questions are asked, no interpretations; just a constant seeking of clarification *of what it means to Vicky.*

UNDERSTANDING ECLECTIC (OR INTEGRATED) COUNSELLING

While many counsellors work to one model of counselling, probably an equal number are eclectic (or integrated) counsellors, using a variety of approaches. They are most likely to have one core framework, but borrow from other models and apply them to suit *your* particular needs.

Purists might not approve of this varied use of theories or models, but eclectic counsellors would possibly counter this with, 'If it will help, use it.' Eclectics would also believe that instead of trying to fit the client into one framework or model, they should be adaptable and find what works for you, rather than the other way round. Every person has needs and goals specific to their own life stage, particular problem(s) or degrees of self-awareness.

Thus a counsellor using an eclectic or integrated approach may use different approaches.

- A psychodynamic approach to bring unconscious drives/and or defences into conscious awareness.

- Behavioural therapy may be appropriate if a particular behaviour pattern is inhibiting you, for example if you have a specific sexual difficulty.

- Cognitive therapy could help if the messages from your earlier life are leading to self-defeating or self-destruction through patterns or behaviours.

- Most counsellors using an eclectic approach, work with the person-centred core principles.

The emphasis of this book is on individual counselling. Sometimes people's first experience of counselling comes when they have marital or relationship problems and they seek counselling together as a way of resolving their difficulties. Because a relationship encompasses two unique individuals whose personalities, needs, and past histories, and degrees of self-awareness may be very different, counsellors work with most couples using an integrated or eclectic approach.

SUMMARISING THE HELPING RELATIONSHIP

Speaking of the essential characteristics of the counselling relationship, Carl Rogers highlights the following questions which counsellors should consider:

- **Trustworthy**. Can I *be* in some way which will be perceived by the other person as trustworthy, as dependable or consistent in some deep sense?

- **Congruent**. Can I be expressive enough as a person so what I am will be communicated unambiguously?

- **Warmth**. Can I let myself experience positive attitudes towards this person, attitudes of warmth, caring, liking, interest, respect?

- **Separate**. Can I be strong enough as a person to be separate from the other?

- **Secure**. Am I secure enough within myself to permit him his separateness?

- **Empathic**. Can I let myself enter fully into the world of his feelings and personal meanings and see these as he does?

- **Accepting**. Can I be accepting of each facet of this person which he presents to me?

- **Non-threatening**. Can I act with sufficient sensitivity in the relationship that my behaviour will not be perceived as a threat?

- **Non-evaluative**. Can I free this client from the threat of external evaluation, from his or her past and my past?

Carl Rogers[6]

WORKING WITH GOALS

You may seek counselling because you feel stuck in a situation from which you can see no way out. You may half-sense a way, but it is obscured. Counselling can help you to develop a sense of direction which often accompanies hope.

Goal-setting is a highly cognitive approach which might not appeal to you, and will not be used by all counsellors. However, learning the skills of goal-setting can have spin-offs in other areas of your life. Goal-setting will take into account feelings and behavioural factors as well as your creative potential.

There is more to helping than talking and planning. If you are to live more effectively you must *act*. When you refuse to act, it means that you are failing to cope with problems in living or do not exploit opportunities. The attainment of goals cannot be left to chance.

Goals should be set neither too low nor too high. Goals set inappropriately high can cause you to feel inadequate; goals set too low do not generate enthusiasm. Goals must be tailored to suit you, because you are unique. Do not be tempted to reach for someone else's goal. Goals also have to be specific, within a time-frame. Goals that are to be accomplished 'sometime or other' are rarely achieved.

One of the great exponents of the need for clear goal-setting in counselling is Gerard Egan, an American psychologist. His proposes the following three-stage model.

Stage 1
The current scenario (where you are now).

Stage 2
The preferred scenario (where you would like to be).

Stage 3
Getting there (developing strategies and plans).

Asking questions about goals
1. What precisely is going wrong?
2. What precisely do I want to change?
3. What behaviours do I want to get rid of?
4. What new behaviours do I want to develop?

5. What are my strengths, and how can I make them work for me?
6. What opportunities have I been ignoring?
7. Are there any people I have been ignoring as resources?
8. Do any of my attitudes, beliefs, opinions work against a positive outcome?
9. Is there anything I am trying to avoid?
10. What will the final outcome be?
11. Is my plan clear, specific and detailed?
12. How can I measure and verify the outcomes?
13. Is my plan realistic?
14. Is my plan genuine and attainable?
15. Can I achieve this within a realistic time frame?
16. What would I do differently with the people in my life?
17. What would I have accomplished?

Summarising goal-setting

- Don't spend 80% of time on something that will only have a 20% reward.

- Work on something that will show a rapid reward, where the benefits outweigh the costs.

- Own the problem. Only when you clearly define and own your problem can you do something about changing it. You do not own the problem all the time you blame other people, outside forces or circumstances. Owning the problem increases your control of it.

- Deal with crises immediately.

- Distinguish problems from symptoms.

- Work on problems which are causing you pain.

- Tackle one specific problem or part of a larger problem.

- Work to change something that will influence other areas of your life.

- Work on something that is obviously visible.

- If other people are involved, the problem is more urgent.

- A chronic problem is like a running sore, it is debilitating. It needs an urgent operation. Don't put it off, hoping it will go away.

- Problems and opportunities that are clearly identified and defined are easier to manage than where exploration just goes aimlessly round and round.

CASE STUDY

Jim chooses to work on his feelings

Jim was a university lecturer in engineering. A man in his mid-30s, with a first-class degree in mathematics and another in engineering, he found it difficult to relate to people. 'I only need to say a few words, but they cut the other person to pieces.' He was intolerant of 'woolly thinking' and 'sentimentality'. His razor-sharp mind, which he used as a weapon, alienated him from people. He had no girlfriend; 'Never know how to relate to them. I need to understand my feelings,' was his reason for coming for counselling.

Over the course of many months, Jim learnt that it was safe to have feelings, rather than using his intellect to shield himself from becoming involved with people. Exploring many issues brought much pain, but also healing. I heard from him six years later. He had changed jobs, was more involved with people, and had a girlfriend. Jim needed to work with his feelings to achieve some sort of balance in his life.

CHOOSING THE BEST APPROACH FOR YOU

There are various ways in which people choose their counsellor and type of counselling. Your GP or another professional may refer you to a particular counsellor; a friend or relation who has had counselling themselves may recommend their counsellor.

As discussed in Chapter 2, you may shop around for the best fit that can be created between you and the counsellor. Some people choose an approach with which they instinctively feel comfortable.

- If you are a thinking person who likes to reason things out, then maybe a counsellor whose main concentration is cognitive counselling will be the one for you.

- If concentrating on feelings is not as easy for you, then you might gain more understanding, self-awareness and growth if you opt for an approach which will be more personally challenging, as the case of Jim shows.

- If you find making decisions and taking action difficult, there could be advantages for working cognitively or behaviourally.

There are other factors which you may need to consider such as: how much do you want to gain insight into yourself and your relationships, or do you want to solve a specific problem? For how long are you prepared to work in the counselling relationship? Would you like your counsellor to be 'there for you' for a length of time, and what are the cost and time implications for you?

The table in Figure 6 gives a general idea of the comparisons between the approaches in terms of:

- time scale
- solution orientation versus self-awareness orientation
- degree of direction/interpretation in the various ways of work-ing.

SUMMARY

1. There are many valid approaches, those introduced here are psychodynamic, behavioural, cognitive and person-centred, and eclectic. Each can help you live your life with more well-being. Knowing something about different approaches is one way of helping you make an informed choice of counsellor. Asking questions before you start might avoid disappointment later, if you find that the particular approach does not suit your personality. However, what you get out of counselling probably rests not so much on the approach or the techniques used, but on the relationship between yourself and the counsellor. In behavioural or cognitive counselling, for example, there might not be as much emphasis on the counsellor working within your frame of reference, yet the relationship can be just as rewarding and the outcome equally positive.

2. A broad distinction can be made between the psychodynamic and person-centred approaches. The psychodynamic approach works with insight related to unconscious material, whereas

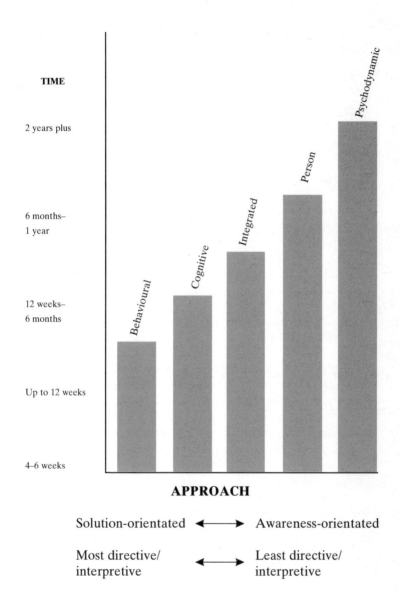

Fig. 6. Relativity of different approaches.

the person-centred counsellor works with insight related to your feelings. If in the process you elicit unconscious material, so be it, but the unconscious is not the focus. The person-centred approach hinges on creating a climate based on the core conditions of empathy, warmth, genuineness and regard. While these are also present in the psychodynamic approach they are not as evident, mainly because the counsellor does not become as involved as a person.

3. In behavioural and cognitive counselling the focus is on creating change. Various techniques and models will be used to assist that change. However, it is change that *you* want, not what the *counsellor* thinks would be best for you which would go against everything counselling stands for. How you think and behave influences how you feel, and vice versa. To help the change process, counsellors of many different persuasions, although not the person-centred counsellor, will use a range of problem-solving skills to help you reach your goal. Skills, techniques and models are not to be despised, and when they are tailored to suit your needs they are of immense value.

4. Deciding that you might benefit from counselling is not something you should rush into, any more than you would rush into buying a car. Spend as much time as you need to explore what counselling means *for you*. Consider the various approaches discussed here; shop around, ask questions. Clients who take time to decide are often the ones who get the most out of counselling.

6

Understanding The Whole Counselling Process

You will get the most out of counselling if you feel fully engaged, and being fully engaged is aided by being aware of what is going on. An analogy can be drawn between nursing and counselling. A nurse can function at different levels; she can do practical tasks to and for the patient, but there is more to nursing than simply carrying out techniques that can be learnt. The nurse has to have a sound knowledge of how the body functions and how one organ relates to another. She cannot see inside the patient, but by careful observation and interpreting the signs she aids the physician in assessing what is wrong with the patient, and when treatment is going according to plan.

The patient too has a role to play, in reporting how he feels and trying to report accurately and precisely. Patients who feel involved in the treatment plan are more likely to be co-operative patients and to recover more quickly, simply because they feel they have had a significant part to play in their own healing. What applies in medicine applies equally in counselling. This chapter will discuss the counselling relationship *from the client's perspective*.

UNDERSTANDING THE COUNSELLING CONTRACT

When you and your counsellor have established that you feel able to work together, it is usual to enter into some form of 'contract' or agreement about how you will proceed. This is particularly important when it seems that more than one session is required.

You may jib at the word 'contract'; but what it does imply is an undertaking, on both sides, of how counselling is to be conducted. You will agree, in broad detail, the purpose of counselling and the area or areas to be tackled, although there may be certain details that you do not wish to touch on, at least until the relationship is firmly established.

Setting boundaries

The contract is a setting of boundaries and expectations. You may not want to set boundaries; you may want counselling to be free-ranging. Such trust places a tremendous onus on the counsellor who, unknowingly, may tread on uncharted land; you, the client, because of some emotional disturbance, may resent this intrusion. Some boundaries are usually helpful.

In addition to the boundaries to exploration, there are the boundaries of time. How long will each session last? How frequently will you meet, and where? In a fee-paying service the fee will be discussed and agreed. There needs to be a tentative agreement reached on how many sessions should be aimed at and how they will be assessed. A part of the contract should be the supervisory relationship that the counsellor has, and its purpose.

Making a contract

While some counsellors work to a verbal contract, others prefer a written agreement, signed by both counsellor and client. *Learning to Counsel* (Jan Sutton and William Stewart) gives an example of a written contract, which covers:

- Confidentiality, which includes the need for supervision.

- The number of sessions and the length of each session.

- Fees.

- Holiday arrangements.

- Termination of counselling before the agreed number of sessions.

- Records kept by the counsellor.

- The use of audio tapes to be agreed.

The British Association for Counselling *Code of Ethics and Practice for Counsellors* says this about contracts:

> Counsellors are responsible for communicating the terms on which counselling is being offered, including availability, the degree of confidentiality offered and their expectations of clients regarding fees, cancelled appointments and any other significant matters. The communication of these terms and any negotiations over these should be concluded before the client incurs any financial liability.

A contract such as this sets out clearly that counselling has a definite structure, that it is every bit as professional as, for example, attending your doctor. Establishing a contract protects both you and the counsellor, and it is at the contract stage that you are encouraged to make any stipulations which the counsellor might not have included.

Some elements of the contract, such as length of sessions, frequency, time-keeping and fees are generally fixed, although fees are often negotiable. How the counselling develops is less fixed.

The contract may also include whether you can contact the counsellor in the case of a crisis or an emergency. Some counsellors agree to telephone contact between sessions, others do not. Try, in the initial session, to get as many answers to your questions as you can; doing so will help you to feel more at ease.

Identifying the difference between counselling and other relationships

Counselling is different from other relationships, in that at all times you are the person in focus. The relationships exists with the express purpose of benefiting you. The relationship between you and your counsellor is a professional one, not personal, just as in the relationship between doctor and patient. It is a therapeutic relationship which has been initiated by you and will come to a more or less predetermined end. While the relationship is one of equals, a partnership, an alliance, it is your needs which always take precedence. When you and the counsellor separate you may never see each other again, unless you resume the relationship for further counselling.

Identifying the qualities and skills counsellors need

It is difficult to distinguish qualities from skills, for often they blend into one another like ingredients in a cake. A second difficulty is that if one listed all the essential qualities it might seem as if the counsellor were some sort of saint or deity. And that is far from the truth. Counsellors are human in all respects, not perfect, but one of their qualities is that they have an insatiable curiosity about life, and a desire to know what makes themselves and other people tick. Their knowledge of personal psychology enables them to relate to a wide range of people.

Your counsellor must be a good listener. Yet listening is not enough, the counsellor has to understand what you are saying, and help you search for the feelings which the words convey, and to be able to communicate this understanding to you in a way that helps you move forward.

Counsellors are independent and secure enough in themselves not to want to use the counselling relationship to satisfy their own personal needs. One of the aims is to empower you to strive to become whatever you wish.

Understanding why the counsellor might need to keep records

Not all counsellors agree about keeping records. Those against question the advisability on grounds of confidentiality. Those in favour are aware that accurate recording aids recall of the session. The counsellor may take notes during the session. If you are anxious about note-taking and record-keeping, this is something you should discuss with the counsellor. Similar to records are the notes the counsellor might make during a session. Not all counsellors make notes or keep detailed records. If you wish to see what your counsellor has written about you, this is one of the questions to ask at the contract stage.

IDENTIFYING SOME ESSENTIAL ELEMENTS IN COUNSELLING

Counselling consists mainly of verbal exchange

This might seem an obvious statement, yet within this is the expectancy that counsellor and client will engage in dialogue. It might seem that only people who are verbally skilled will benefit from counselling, and that people less skilled might not.

It is certainly true that counselling training demands a high level of verbal skill, but verbal fluency does not equate with being able to express one's feelings. Feelings are very often expressed in simple terms. In fact, the more articulate a person is, the more difficult they might find expressing feelings. If you feel handicapped at not being articulate, please do not be put off from seeking counselling. One of the skills of most counsellors is that of helping you express yourself.

You have the right to choose the direction of your own life

It would be arrogant and patronising for the counsellor even to think that he or she knew what was best for you. It is difficult enough for most of us to manage our own lives let alone presume to tell other people how they should live theirs.

Self-direction or self-determination – one of the fundamental principles in counselling – is your basic right of freedom to choose your own direction, even though that decision may clash with the values, beliefs and desires of other people. You, and you alone, have the responsibility to live your own life and achieve life's goals as you perceive them.

Your counsellor will help you mobilise your inner resources so that you are more able to make balanced decisions. You may feel helpless to make decisions because the alternatives are unclear. Helping you tease out what is involved is often all that is necessary to enable you to make a decision and to take responsibility for what you decide to do.

The counsellor helps you clear some of the mist away from the window, thus allowing you to look out and see a little more clearly. However, for every individual right of choice there are accompanying duties and responsibilities in your relationship with others. When you practise self-determination it does not mean that you are indifferent to the needs of other people. In choosing your own direction you have to be careful that you do not trample on the rights of other people.

Counselling is a highly confidential relationship

The preservation of confidential information is a basic right of the client and an ethical obligation upon the counsellor. If you were asked what is your understanding of 'confidentiality' you would probably say that you didn't want the details of what you disclosed gossiped about or discussed with people who didn't have to be involved. You would probably agree that the counsellor, where necessary, would be free to discuss broad details with professional colleagues, but only after your prior consent had been obtained.

Most counsellors at some time in their careers have been faced with the painful decision of whether or not to respect confidence or, for the good of society or to prevent something disastrous happening, to break it. Whatever is decided, no action should be taken without discussion with you.

Confidentiality is two-way. Just as the counsellor respects your privacy, there is an obligation on you to respect the counsellor's privacy and whatever the counsellor discloses about him or herself, or what you glean about the counsellor from the relationship. What you tell other people about the counselling is your prerogative provided it does not break the confidential relationship you have with your counsellor.

The British Association for Counselling (BAC) lays down a strict code of ethics for its members, although not all counsellors are members. (Membership of this or any other body is not yet a legal requirement in Britain.) Confidentiality provides you, the client, with safety and privacy, and any doubts about confidentiality will seriously interfere with what you reveal.

Nothing your counsellor says, writes or in any way communicates to a third party should identify who are you. Check out the counsellor's boundaries of confidentiality, and under what circumstances he/she would break them and how this would be done. The counsellor might be able to give you a copy of the BAC or other code of ethics/practice adhered to.

Motivation increases the benefits

Clients who are motivated to seek counselling are more likely to benefit from it than those who are pressed into it. 'What you need is counselling,' said Anne, to her teenaged son, 'I'll make an appointment for you.' Stan came, and was resentful. So one of the first things was to acknowledge that resentment. That was one counsellor's experience.

'I would like you to see my wife,' said the caller. I listened to him for a few minutes before saying, 'I can appreciate that you feel your wife would benefit from seeing me, and thank you for that confidence. What I suggest is that your wife phones me and we can make arrangements.' My policy is that I do not take appointments made on someone else's behalf.

If someone is pressuring you into going for counselling, you are likely to feel resentful and undermined. Certainly this is something you ought to discuss with the counsellor, for you could feel that they are acting as an agent of control and that could lead to an unproductive relationship.

The counsellor has respect for the client's unique individuality

This has been touched upon several times. When the counsellor recognises and respects your uniqueness, this means accepting you not just as a human being but as *this* human being – just as you are. You have the need and the right to be related to as unique. You need the counsellor's undivided attention and privacy to be able to discuss your unique problem. When your uniqueness is respected you will respond by giving information and disclosing feelings. When you are related to with uniqueness, when you feel understood, you will enter more willingly into the helping relationship.

HIGHLIGHTING THE MAIN ASPECTS OF THE COUNSELLING PROCESS

1. Getting on your wavelength.
2. Active listening and appropriate responding.
3. Remaining impartial and suspending judgement.
4. Using the skills of:

   Attending. The counsellor gives full attention to what you are saying: the facts, the feelings and the accompanying body language. Just as the counsellor attends to you, your task is to attend to the counsellor.
   Paraphrasing the content. Paraphrasing lets you hear what you said through someone else's words, often bringing clarification. If the counsellor's paraphrase doesn't sound accurate, try to correct it rather than let it slide.
   Reflecting feelings. Like paraphrasing, the counsellor reflects your feelings. By bringing them into the open you will be able to acknowledge them. If the feelings are not accurate, say so, and thus reach firmer understanding of what your feelings are.
   Open questions. Many counsellors steer clear of any form of questioning, which gives the impression of probing. Open questions are phrased in such a way that you are encouraged to continue talking, rather than replying with a yes or a no.
   Summarising. From time to time the counsellor will create little islands, in which what has taken place is summarised. This gives you an opportunity to take stock of where you have come from, what has been said, the feelings, and any major issues covered. Some counsellors invite their clients to summarise and this is a useful exercise.
   Focusing. As the word implies, the counsellor will help to focus your attention on, for example, two contrasting ideas, feelings, statements, or possibilities; listing the main issues and asking you to concentrate on one; choosing what he or

she considers the main issue. This is like putting part of your overall problem under the microscope.

Challenging. If you are confused or uncertain you may present conflict or contradictory ideas or statements, or even contradictory feelings. The counsellor will draw attention to such contradictions, as a way to help you find a way through the confusion.

Self-disclosure. The counsellor may decide to disclose something about him or herself. This is not to take the focus from you, but is often a way to illustrate a particular point.

Immediacy. Counselling is more effective when working in the present, what is called the 'here and now'; where feelings can be dealt with, rather than relating feelings that happened in the past. It also means tackling feelings that are generated between you and the counsellor.

Concreteness. This means that the counsellor helps you to clarify what you want to say. When we are confused or unclear, what we want to say doesn't always come out clearly enough. A second point is that if you are under stress, what you want to say is fudged by generalisations and vague statements. Helping you be concise and clear is part of the counsellor's task.

Waiting for a reply. Counselling is not 'ordinary' conversation. If you are struggling to express your deep feelings you could be put off if the counsellor hurried you. This waiting is important.

The constructive use of silences. Silences are an essential part of any conversation, yet some people feel threatened and unnerved by silence. Do you? Much happens in the silence, as both you and the counsellor give each other time to reflect on what is happening.

Keeping pace with the client. At all times it is you who leads; the counsellor accompanies, walks alongside. If you need to retrace your steps, not once but many times, the counsellor will go with you. You set the pace, not the counsellor.

Reading between the lines. This is not clairvoyance, or anything spooky; it is the skill of accurate listening and of accurate empathy.

Demonstrating the principles of the counselling relationship:
- Respecting your uniqueness.
- Respecting, reflecting and exploring your feelings.
- Being willing to become engaged, but not over-involved.

- Encouraging your self-direction.
- Respecting confidentiality.
- Acceptance.
- Being non-judgemental.

Being able to enter your frame of reference.

Demonstrating accurate empathy.

Keeping the interview moving forward. It might sound paradoxical, but helping you move forward might mean looking back. If you feel stuck (or the counsellor may feel stuck) then looking back, clarifying where you have come from and what was discovered on the way often provides impetus for moving forward.

Keeping objective when planning action. The action stage of counselling does not necessarily always come at the end, although it is usually so associated. One of the aims of counselling might be to help you take action – now, not at some future time. But one of the difficulties you might face is that although you want to take action, you are uncertain what it could or should be. The counsellor will help you explore various options, so that you can take what you feel is the most appropriate action for you. The counsellor will not try to influence your decision, although he or she may open up different scenarios, so that you can make a more informed choice.

Exploring why counselling is more than listening

Many people say of counselling, 'All you have to do is be a good listener.' This is only half the truth. Counselling involves you and counsellor in listening and talking. If the aim of counselling is to encourage you to talk about something that is troubling you, then it is obvious that the counsellor must be a listener. Effective listening in counselling is an active process of hearing what you say and what you are trying to say: it certainly is not a passive soaking up of everything you say without responding. It is a careful monitoring of the words to try and understand their contextual meaning and the underlying feelings.

Active listening means the counsellor:

- hearing and responding to what you have said, in a way that demonstrates that you have been heard

- giving you full and undivided attention

- taking an interest in what you are saying

- hearing your feelings conveyed by your words, not just the words themselves

- being aware of your body language.

Counselling is not normal conversation. In counselling you, and you alone, are the focus. Within that relationship you know the time is yours to use as you want, to say what you want, and all the time knowing that you are being listened to. Such listening enhances your self-esteem, for it reinforces that you are a person of worth, and people who feel valued are more open to change.

In normal conversation you have without doubt had the experience of not being listened to, of your feelings not being heard as if the other person is emotionally tone-deaf. Here are some of the ways you may not be listened to in normal conversation. You might find it useful to think if you are also guilty of any of these.

- not paying attention

- pretend-listening

- listening but not hearing the meaning

- rehearsing what to say

- interrupting the speaker in mid-sentence

- hearing what is expected

- feeling defensive, expecting an attack

- listening for something to disagree with.

In the counselling relationship, you have to listen to the counsellor so some or all of the eight points above might apply. Also, you might experience difficulty when strong emotions are present; it is as if they switch off your emotional hearing aid. Have you ever had the experience of walking down the street after hearing bad news and not hearing someone speak to you? That will give you an insight into what might happen in counselling. The counsellor will be alert to when you have not heard what has been said. Then you have to make a choice, to respond to what the counsellor has said, or to disclose the feelings that are uppermost.

If you are able to say, 'What you said triggered off this strong feeling in me' you are then dealing with the here and now feelings, but you may need time to mull them over. Perhaps they are not ready for discussion, now or ever. Try not to be pressed into talking about feelings if you are not ready.

EXPERIENCING RESISTANCE DURING COUNSELLING

Even though you are a willing partner in counselling, you may still experience resistance to it. This paradox is something which every counsellor recognises and accepts. You are likely to avoid something, in the first instance, because of what is happening within you. Conflict of any kind creates its own resistance. Another reason for resistance is linked with the feeling of not being master of your own ship. Disappointment, fear, resentment, frustration and anger are feelings which are all liable to be present. You may realise that your personal life is in chaos and your inner world in turmoil. Guilt might be causing you to anticipate censure which leads to a build-up of resistance.

Anticipated change may also cause resistance within you. The very fact that you are in counselling carries with it the implication that some change is likely, and almost inevitable. But change can be for the better, and is not always a harbinger of fear. While you may agree that change is required, indeed is desirable, paradoxically you may be resisting the change.

In a sense this is related to your perception of the counsellor. If you see the counsellor as someone who can enforce change, you may show more resistance than if you regard him or her as a person who will enable you to make your own changes. If you do not accept that you have a problem you will almost certainly be resistant. But as we have already said, not all counselling is problem-focused. Even if you are in counselling for personal development, and do not have a problem to focus on, you may still experience resistance because of subtle changes taking place within you.

Understanding resistance

Resistance might arise from a departure by the counsellor from the agreed contract. Part of that contract might have been that you do not want to discuss a particular topic, and if you detect that the exploration is heading that way, you would naturally resist. Similarly, if you feel that the exploration is heading too quickly in a certain direction, you may want to pull back.

If you feel a resistance, try to express it to the counsellor. You may not use that particular word, but a useful way is to express it as an image. Something like, 'I seem to have come up against a brick wall, and I don't want to go any further at the moment,' will let the counsellor glimpse what you are feeling and will let you back off.

You may think that if you experience resistance you are not being a good client. It is doubtful if your counsellor would expect you to be a 'good' client. Being good implies that you do what is expected of you and has echoes of trying to win approval. More constructive than hoping to be good, and pleasing the counsellor, is to try to be open about your feelings. This is tied up with being able to trust your feelings, as well as having confidence to express them and in the counsellor's ability to understand you.

You may find it difficult to trust, for example, if your self-esteem is at a low ebb, or if you feel a failure. And not being able to trust might mean that you resist what the counsellor is reflecting or exploring. Part of that resistance may arise from a feeling that circumstances are pushing you into counselling against your will. You may resist counselling because it is new and strange. Rather than striving to be a good client, try to work as a partner with the counsellor.

UNDERSTANDING THE THERAPEUTIC HOUR

This section includes several related points – questions you might want to ask, and questions which some other clients have asked.

How long will counselling last?

There are two questions here: the length of each session, and how long counselling will last overall. Most counsellors work to what is called the 'therapeutic hour' or '50 minute hour'. This allows the counsellor time to make any notes before seeing the next client; beyond this time, efficiency begins to drop off rapidly.

Most counsellors advise a time limit, and certainly during training this aspect is always stressed. Counselling can be emotionally draining and exhausting. The knowledge that there is a time limit can be a positive safeguard for both you and the counsellor.

After one or two sessions, you yourself learn to draw the

interview to a close. You also may feel less anxious if you know there is a time limit; it also gives a sense of urgency to the interview which can be positively helpful. If the session has been well structured, you will instinctively feel when the counsellor is starting to draw to a close. This stage is important, for you are able, mentally, to pick up the threads ready to move out into the 'real' world. A clock strategically placed is an aid to the counsellor, and 'I see time is just about up' alerts you to the ending. Some counsellors will say something like, 'I see time is almost up, let's summarise.' Others will simply say that time is up and the session is over.

How long will counselling last over a period? People are not clients for life. Right from the start, in establishing the contract, you and the counsellor set boundaries. One of those is the number of sessions to which you commit yourself, though usually with the proviso of either opting out of or extending the contract.

Why is time so important?

Having a stated time is an important boundary of the relationship. As with all appointments, time has its place. As a set time is a part of the contract the counsellor expects that you will arrive and leave on time. If you arrive late, the counsellor might not be able to give you the full time if another client is expected.

What if I think of something important just as the session is ending?

This is a difficult one, and it is certainly something you might want to discuss with your counsellor before it happens. In counselling circles this phenomenon is known as the 'hand on the door' – the client, just leaving, halts and discloses something quite dramatic. This immediately thrusts the counsellor on the horns of a dilemma – to extend the time or leave the disclosure hanging around for another week.

Leaving something to the end might indicate that you may be afraid to reveal it, or you may not have developed enough trust, particularly in the early stages of counselling. Is it that you are seeking more of the counsellor's time? Has the disclosure really only come to mind? Have you been trying to pluck up courage and the counsellor has not picked this up? Do you really want to discuss it?

Whatever the reason, the counsellor has to make a decision – continue with the session or close it. The counsellor may say something like, 'I heard what you said, however, our time has gone, we will explore it next time if you wish.' This leaves you knowing that the counsellor did hear, and the matter is clearly in your control.

CASE STUDY

Meg heads for the door

Meg was a counsellor, coming to me for personal therapy as part of her training. In the fourth session we had been discussing a particular issue. As we were closing the session I said to Meg, 'What would you take away with you from today?' Meg said, 'My supervisor suggested I talk to you about my feelings with the training group.' We both laughed; she and I knew that that was a beautiful demonstration of the 'hand on the door phenomenon'. The following week we did discuss it, and the reason for waiting until the last minute. Meg freely admitted that the feelings she needed to discuss were too raw and she needed time to sort them out.

BEING REFERRED TO ANOTHER COUNSELLOR

No counsellor can be all things to all clients. While the ability to relate with all the core conditions is one thing, having experience in specific fields or expertise is something different. An analogy can be drawn from medicine. GPs have a great deal of experience in many different areas of medicine, but they often have to refer patients to specialists; just so in counselling.

Some counsellors have specialised in marriage and family therapy, others in drug and alcohol abuse; people who have been sexually abused; people who suffer from eating disorder; mental illness.

The counsellor you choose may, as counselling progresses, feel that you need more specialised help. Just as a GP will discuss with you the need for a specialist opinion, so will the counsellor. Counsellors have a wide network of contacts, and after discussion your counsellor will make arrangements for you to meet, although the final decision invariably rests with you.

What if you can't get on with your counsellor?

Two fundamentals of counselling are being open and genuine. This applies equally to you as well as the counsellor. If you cannot work with your chosen counsellor, then the choice is yours – to discontinue or to confront the issue. If you are able to be open and tell the counsellor how you feel, you both have a wonderful opportunity to arrive at a deeper understanding of your relationship. Doing this provides an opportunity for growth for both of you.

SAYING GOODBYE

Counselling is like taking a journey. We know from where we have come and roughly the route taken, but on looking back, the starting point has become obscured, partly through distance but also through time.

Unlike a journey, it is necessary for both you and your counsellor to look back in order to firmly establish the final position. Looking back to where and why the journey began many prove difficult; feelings, as well as memories, fade with time. Looking back is not always comfortable. It may reveal obstacles not previously recognised. Time spent on questions like those which follow will reinforce that counselling has been a real partnership.

Looking back along the counselling road

- What different problems did we identify and how were these tackled?

- What goals did I set and how far have I achieved them?

- What specific areas of growth and insights did I achieve?

- What do I still need to achieve?

- What other resources do I need to help me move forward?

- Do I feel able to tell the counsellor how I feel about ending?

- What are the positives about the counselling experience?

- What are the negatives about the counselling experience?

- What is my overall assessment of the counselling relationship?

- Do I feel confident that I could re-enter counselling in the future?

How will you know if counselling has been successful?

If you have stayed the course, have set goals and reached some of them, have achieved some insight and have more self-awareness, and are more able to manage your life, then is this not success?

But success and failure are two sides of the same coin, and counsellors will seldom talk in terms of one or the other.

Roy was a youth counsellor. Andrew, one of his constant clients, was never able to hold down a job. Roy spent several hours with Andrew, and many times he helped him get jobs and with frequent regularity Andrew appeared, jobless, for another 'chat'. In one of his jobless periods he stole a car, crashed it and was killed.

Did Roy go wrong somewhere? Was there something he could have done? Some stop he could have pulled out? Some technique he could have used to prevent this tragedy?

Andrew had a choice. Nothing 'made' him steal that car; it was his choice. It is certainly true that he may have cried loud and long for help and perhaps Roy did not hear him. When the news of Andrew's death was broken to Roy, he was distressed to think that maybe he had not done all he could to help Andrew. This is a natural question to ask. It had the effect of making him stop and re-evaluate: that was positive and constructive. But for Roy to have taken on his shoulders the responsibility for Andrew's actions would have been burdening himself unfairly, and most certainly would seriously have affected his counselling.

Saying goodbye constructively
Counselling is no ordinary relationship. You have shared your story with an almost complete stranger, chosen not for his or her friendship but for a very specific purpose. Together you have journeyed, explored, shared, laughed and possibly cried. You have felt free to be yourself, possibly like in no other relationship. You have been accepted for who you are, without reservation or criticism. You have been angry, maybe furious with this person who has given you unconditional love. You have seen yourself through the eyes of another, whose wisdom has rubbed off on you. Now it is time to say goodbye. You may never see this person again. This might be a moment of sadness, yet within the relationship this has been a moment to which you have worked. Now you journey alone, yet with the memory and the experience of having been accompanied part-way. The time you and your counsellor have spent together was not an end in itself, it was but a means. Draw on the experience, for you will have learnt many things about yourself, you will have acquired insights and skills. Use

them constructively in your own life and, wherever possible, use them to enhance the life of other people.

SUMMARY

1. Counselling, in keeping with other forms of psychological therapy, is unlike any other relationship. No other relationship holds you so much in cupped hands, enfolding you in warmth which does not threaten or invade where the other person is totally available, albeit for a limited time; where you are listened to with total acceptance free from judgement; where you are the focus of caring attention and your needs are all that matter. Although counsellors may fall short of that some of the time, this is the ideal towards which the counsellor strives.

2. The counsellor uses a battery of relationship skills which focus on accurate listening and responding, aiming to establish and maintain effective communication between you and the counsellor. You may feel that your communication skills are less than adequate, if so, try not to let that stop you engaging in counselling. If you are able to relate how you feel, then that is one of the main avenues of communication.

3. Being the focus of the counselling relationship might be off-putting at times, like being centre-stage with the spotlight showing up your every movement. Even though you are always in focus, the counsellor is not like some expectant spider waiting to pounce on you and tear you apart. Your counsellor walks alongside you, encouraging you to take one more step along the road towards self-discovery, or whatever goal you have set yourself.

4. Trusting your counsellor with a particular feeling, experience, memory, or insight might not always be easy and you may resist or avoid. Trust cannot be demanded; it has to be earned. The more accurately your counsellor understands you, relates to you with empathy, listens to your words and feelings and responds in such a way that you are encouraged to continue, the more will trust develop between you.

5. Enjoy your counselling. Yes, there are serious times ahead, and there are likely to be tears, struggles and pain, for there is no growth without them. But there will be happy moments, times when you and the counsellor can laugh and rejoice as maybe you recall events long-since forgotten, or as you achieve insights that brighten the session, as you experience liberation from memories and feelings that have haunted you, maybe for years.

CONCLUSION

Counselling is like a journey. You start, continue and reach the end. You can look back in your mind's eye and see whence you came, the road travelled, the obstacles overcome, the wonderful sights seen, the people you met and journeyed with. There will be highlights that will forever be etched on your memory. You may have seen a wonderful sunrise or sunset, with all its silver and gold hues. You may have travelled through rain and seen a glorious rainbow, or heard the song of the early-morning blackbird. You may have become footsore and weary, at times to the point of exhaustion. You may have wished for a passing vehicle to pick you up and carry you away, to save your aching limbs.

All of these images are similes of what might have happened in counselling, as you and your counsellor have journeyed on what, for both of you, was a momentous experience.

If you have walked the coast-to-coast road, you will know when you have arrived. That is the end of one journey. But there will be other walks to challenge you. Just so in this journey called self-awareness. If you have achieved a little bit of insight, or acquired one single skill to make your life easier, then your self-awareness has been developed that bit more.

Keep alive in your mind and heart the memories of the times you laughed and cried, for they are part of the same experience.

Don't let it stop there. Use the insights and skills you have developed through counselling to lead you on to further exploration. Above all, let these insights and skills not only help you make sense of your own life, but may you pass on something of what you have experienced to benefit other people.

Glossary

A-type personality. An ingrained pattern of behaviour observed in people who struggle to obtain something from their environment as quickly as possible. What they strive for is often not clear and may be in conflict with other things or persons. A-type people are rushed, competitive, aggressive and over-committed to achieving. They are often workaholics.

Acceptance. The feeling of being accepted as we really are, including our strengths and weaknesses, differences of opinions, no matter how unpleasant or uncongenial, without censure. It is not judging someone from a pre-determined set of values.

Empathy. The action of understanding, being aware of, being sensitive to, and getting in touch with the feelings, thoughts and experience of another person.

Genuineness. The degree to which we are freely and deeply ourselves, and are able to relate to people in a sincere and undefensive manner. Also referred to as authenticity, congruence, truth, genuineness it is the precondition for empathy and unconditional positive regard.

Insight. In psychological terms, the discovery by an individual of the psychological connection between earlier and later events so as to lead to recognition of the roots of a particular conflict or conflicts.

Psychoanalysis. A theoretical system of psychology based on the work of Sigmund Freud. Psychoanalysis may be defined as human nature interpreted in terms of conflict. The mind is understood as an expression of conflicting forces – some conscious, the majority unconscious.

Psychodynamic. The study of human emotions as they influence behaviour. Psychodynamic theory recognises the role of the unconscious, and assumes that behaviour is determined by past experience, genetic endowment and current reality. A psychodynamic counsellor works towards the client achieving insight.

Self-awareness. Being aware of our thoughts, feelings and behaviour, as influenced by our traits, values, attitudes, motives, memories and the effect these have on other people.

Self-esteem. A confidence and satisfaction in oneself, self-respect. The value we place on ourselves. A high self-esteem is a positive value; a low self-esteem results from attaching negative values to ourselves or some part of ourselves.

Stress. The adverse internal and behavioural responses to one or more influences which have physical, emotional or social origins. Stress is something strenuous and wearing which a person experiences as a result of something he or she is doing or is being done to them. The feeling of just being tired, jittery or ill are subjective sensations of stress.

Unconditional regard. A quality in counselling where the counsellor demonstrates total acceptance. A non-possessive caring and acceptance of the client, irrespective of how offensive the client's behaviour might be.

Warmth. This is one of the essential qualities in counselling. For warmth to be genuine, it must spring from an attitude of friendliness towards others. It feels comfortable; is liberating; is non-demanding. It melts the coldness and softens the hardness within our hearts.

References

1. M. Friedman, *Touchstones of Reality* (E. P. Dutton, New York 1972).
2. Carl Rogers, *On Becoming a Person: A therapist's view of psychotherapy* (Constable, London 1961).
3. Carl Gustav Jung, *The Integration of the Personality* (1939, p. 285).
4. Carl Rogers in L. Knatsh and A. Wolf (eds), *A Psychotherapist's Casebook: Therapy and technique in practice* (Jossey-Bass, San Francisco 1986).
5. D. Mearns and B. Thorne, *Person-Centred Counselling in Action* (Sage Publications 1988).
6. Carl Rogers, *op. cit.*

Further Reading

A-Z of Counselling Theory and Practice, William Stewart (Stanley Thornes, 1997 2nd edition).

Building Self-esteem: How to replace self-doubt with confidence and well-being, William Stewart (How To Books, 1998).

Cognitive-Behavioural Counselling in Action, Peter Trower, Andrew Casey and Windy Dryden (Sage, 1992).

Controlling Anxiety: How to master your fears and start living with confidence, William Stewart (How To Books, 1998).

Dictionary of Images and Symbols in Counselling, William Stewart (Jessica Kingsley, 1998).

Feel the Fear and Do it Anyway, Susan Jeffers, (Rider Books, London).

Imagery and Symbolism in Counselling, William Stewart (Jessica Kingsley, 1996).

Individual Therapy, Windy Dryden (ed) (Sage Publications, 1996).

Learning to Thrive on Stress: How to build confidence and make pressures work for you, Jan Sutton (How To Books, 1997).

Person-Centred Counselling in Action, David Mearns and Brian Thorne (Sage, 1988).

Psychodynamic Counselling in Action, Michael Jacobs (Sage, 1992).

On Becoming a Person, Carl Rogers (Constable, 1961, reprinted 1986).

Questions and Answers on Counselling in Action, Windy Dryden (ed) (Sage Publications, 1994).

Self-Counselling: How to develop the skills and the insights to positively manage your life, William Stewart (How To Books, 1998).

Self Help for your Nerves, Claire Weekes (Angus & Robertson, 1962).

Super Confidence: The woman's guide to getting what you want out of life, Gael Lindenfield (Thorsons, 1989).

The Road Less Travelled, M. Scott Peck (Arrow Books, 1985).

Useful Addresses

British Association for Counselling, 1 Regent Place, Rugby, Warwickshire CV21 2PJ. Tel: (01788) 578328.

British Association of Psychotherapists, 37 Mapesbury Road, London NW2 4HJ. Tel: (020) 8452 9823.

British Association of Sexual and Marital Therapists, PO Box No 13686, London SW20 92H. Tel: (020) 8543 2707.

Centre for Stress Management, 156 Westcombe Hill, London SE3 7DH. Tel: (020) 8293 4114.

CRUSE (bereavement care), Cruse House, 126 Sheen Road, Richmond, Surrey TW9 1UR. Tel: (020) 8332 7227.

Depression Alliance, 35 Westminster Bridge Road, London SE1 7TB. Tel: (020) 7633 0557.

Institute of Counselling, Clinical and Pastoral Counselling, 6 Dixon Street, Glasgow G1 4AX. Tel: (0141) 204 2230. In addition to many distance learning counselling courses, the Institute offers Psychology for Counsellors, and An Introduction to Stress Management which includes a relaxation instruction tape.

Institute of Family Therapy, 24–32 Stephenson Way, London N1 2HX. Tel: (020) 7391 9150.

Miscarriage Association, Head Office, c/o Clayton Hospital, Northgate, Wakefield, West Yorkshire WF1 3JS. Tel: (01924) 200799.

National Council for One Parent Families, 255 Kentish Town Road, London NW5 2LX. Tel: (020) 7267 1361.

RELATE Marriage Guidance, National Headquarters, Herbert Gray College, Little Church Street, Rugby CV21 3AP. Tel: (01788) 573241.

Samaritans. For your nearest branch consult your local telephone directory.

The Association for Post-Natal Illness, 7 Cowen Avenue, Fulham, London S26 6RH. Tel: (020) 7386 0868.

United Kingdom Council for Psychotherapy, 167–169 Great Portland Street, London W1N 4HJ.

Index